D1099069

Intercultural Business

Arthur H. Bell, Ph.D.
Professor, Management Communication
McLaren School of Business
University of San Francisco

Gary G. Williams, Ph.D.
Dean, McLaren School of Business
University of San Francisco

Illustrated by Deborah Zemke

BARRON'S

All inquiries should be addressed to:
Barron's Educational Series, Inc.
250 Wireless Boulevard
Hauppauge, NY 11788
http://www.barronseduc.com

Library of Congress Catalog Card No. 99-29822

International Standard Book No. 0-7641-1113-2

Library of Congress Cataloging-in-Publication Data
Bell, Arthur H. (Arthur Henry), 1946–
    Intercultural business / by Arthur H. Bell and Gary G. Williams.
      p.   cm. — (Business success series)
    Includes bibliographical references and index.
    ISBN 0-7641-1113-2
    1. Success in business. 2. Intercultural communication.
  I. Williams, Gary G. II. Title. III. Series.
  HF5386.B372   1999
  658′.049—dc21   99-29822
                                      CIP

PRINTED IN HONG KONG
9 8 7 6 5 4 3 2 1

Contents

DEDICATION

Art Bell dedicates this book to his wife Dayle Smith

Gary Williams dedicates this book to his wife Maryann Noble

Acknowledgments

In writing this book, we have drawn upon a wealth of firsthand cultural information from businesspeople throughout the world. We are deeply grateful to all the international managers and executives, named throughout these pages, who have contributed specific suggestions for doing business successfully in their countries.

We are equally thankful for the more general insights shared with us by the following distinguished individuals.

Charanjeet Ajmani
Makoto Asabuki, Japan Center for Intercultural Communications
Ing. Sergio Autrey, Casa Autrey, S.A. de. C.V.
Guillaume van Berchem, Jean Michel Berger & Cie
Payson Cha, HKR International Ltd.
Frozen Products Public Co., Ltd.
Thiraphong Chansiri, Thai Union
Victor Chu, Victor Chu & Co.
Jin-Hwan Chun, LG Group
Dr. Jang-Ho Chung, LG Telecom, Ltd.
Tae Young Chung, Hyunda; Precision America, Inc.
John Fisher, Asia Pacific Brands LLC
Peter Foo, Peninsula Holdings Inc.
Anthony Gaw, Pioneer Industries International Holdings Limited
Nurit Gery
Randolph Guthrie, Beaufort Hotels
George Hara, Data Control Ltd.
Nobutaro Hara, Kokuyo Co. Ltd./HRF

Gary Harilela, The Harilela Group
Junichi Hattori, Seiko Instruments, Inc.
Jason Hou, ELSI Taiwan Language Schools
Ahmed Ismail
Ayca Katun
Billy Kim, Irving Enterprises, Inc.
Jeon Kap-Lee, Hyundai Group
Kimun Lee, Resources Consolidated
David Livdahl, Graham & James Ltd.
Ming Xuan Liu, China Resources (Holding) Co., Ltd.
Putra Masagung, Guthrie GTS, Ltd.
Gregory J. Meadows, Sukhothai Hotel
Jan Melson, Butterfield & Butterfield
Sirin Nimmanahaeminda
Carlos Nuñez Urquiza, Banamex
Peter Palacek, Arthur D. Little International, Inc.
Asad Qizilbash
Young Il Park
Dr. Elton See Tan, America California Bank
Lip-Bu Tan, Walden International Investment Groups
Michael Tao, Kou Feng Industrial Co., Ltd.
Suthie Tejavibulya, Hiang Seng Fibre Container Co., Ltd.
Anka Turner
Peter Underwood, IRC Ltd.
Lucien Wong, Allen & Gledhill
Albert Yu, China Times

In addition, we recognize here our colleagues at the McLaren School of Business, University of San Francisco, and past colleagues and friends at Stanford University, Georgetown University, and the University of Southern California, who have been generous with their expertise and advice.

Preface

Fitting a large topic—in this case, *doing business with the world*—into a short book tempts authors to generalize about and oversimplify the complex cultures of other nations. But pat answers to complicated problems quickly prove misleading for businesspeople preparing for global commerce. Therefore, we have tried our best not to resort to neat but distorting summaries of "what Koreans believe" and "what Mexicans value." (By comparison, we would all hold suspect any quick summary of "what Americans believe and value." We know the complexities of American business culture, and we should expect a similar degree of complexity abroad.)

In place of oversimplifications of cultural values, we offer specific suggestions for adapting successfully to the *cultural expectations* of major (and some minor) trading nations. Where possible, these suggestions appear in the actual words of managers and executives who have spent their business lives in the cultures of which they write. In addition, we gather here a toolbox for the international businessperson: contact information for business information available through foreign embassies in the United States as well as U.S. embassies abroad; a reading list of recent books on doing business in major trading nations; a guide to organizations providing in-person and on-line training for intercultural business relations, and more.

We welcome your comments and suggestions as you apply the insights of this book and make discoveries of your own in your international business experiences. Should this book see further editions, we will be pleased to consider your insights as valued additions. Please contact us at the following e-mail addresses.

Arthur H. Bell, Ph.D. Gary G. Williams, Ph.D.
bell@usfca.edu williamsg@usfca.edu

Introduction

You may already have plane tickets in hand for a business trip abroad. If so, you're probably looking for specific hints on how to meet, greet, and do business successfully with a group of foreign professionals. This book serves your needs.

Or you may be contemplating business relationships outside your own borders (or, for that matter, in the Chinatowns, Japantowns, and other cultural enclaves within your country). You want to know how you can gain competitive advantage by having a cultural "in" with vendors and clients whose culture is new to you. This book answers your questions.

Finally, you may be a student, a manager-in-training, or a manager responsible for the training of others. You recognize that the global business environment of the new century has no place for "the Ugly American," parochial attitudes, and stubborn ignorance about other cultures. This book opens windows to reveal aspects of other cultures that matter most for business success.

Chapter 1

Why Culture Matters

WHAT IS CULTURE?

We could cite a standard definition for *culture:* "the complex whole that includes knowledge, belief, art, law, morals, customs, and any other capabilities and habits acquired by humans as members of society." But such a cumbersome definition is a bit like the captain of the *Titanic* defining *iceberg* as "a combination of hydrogen and oxygen cooled to below 32 degrees Fahrenheit." He might better have defined *iceberg* as "that big thing DEAD AHEAD!"

Culture in global business practice has the same urgency and potential consequences as the iceberg that the *Titanic* struck. Cultural mistakes can (and do) sink business ships each day. For that reason, here's our working definition of *culture: "what is expected by the populace of a given country or region."*

THE FEEL OF CULTURE

Try this quick experiment. Take out a pen and sign your typical business signature. Now put the pen in your other hand and attempt to sign your name again. For this second signature, were you able to form the letters legibly? Probably so. But it felt funny— you were trying something that went against years of practice and experience. Signing your name with your "wrong" hand felt awkward, labored, and uncomfortable.

That's precisely how many businesspeople feel when they experience a new culture for the first time. "That's a strange way to run a meeting," you may find yourself thinking. Or "it feels funny" to conclude a business deal on a verbal agreement rather than with the signing of a formal contract.

These feelings of awkwardness and discomfort are not yours alone, of course. Your foreign hosts may feel equally ill-at-ease as you impose U.S. assumptions and habits on business relations. For example, they may wonder why you failed to bring an appropriate gift to your first meeting with their business leader. They may be put off by your eagerness to talk business over lunch or dinner. They may consider your negotiating style rude and ineffective.

It's less than helpful to say that these foreign business associates do not share your cultural values. In fact, your most important values are shared by people around the world: your feelings toward family and friends, your need for personal security and happiness, your desire for a better future, and your love of country, for example.

You aren't feeling awkward or confused in a new culture due to differences in values so much as differences in *expectations*. For example, take a queue of Londoners waiting for a bus. Just because the English form a line at their bus stops (unlike the American free-for-all), can we conclude that the English value order and civility more than Americans? Not when we observe these same Brits crowding the entry gates at a football (soccer) stadium.

Understanding another culture means knowing and respecting its expectations much more than theorizing about its core values. It's often the case that your foreign business hosts may not be able to defend or account for their expectations on the basis of any particular set of values. "It's just the way we do things here," comes their explanation. Like signing one's signature, it feels right one way and wrong another way.

The focus of this short book, then, is on what others expect of you when you visit their cultures for business purposes. The reasons behind these expectations are often complex beyond knowing—an age-old mixture of historical, religious, aesthetic, political, and even genetic causes. Our business here is not to propound vague and unprovable theories about what the Chinese, French, Germans, or Japanese value. Instead, we will target much more practical and answerable questions: What do other trading cultures expect in

◆ written communications?

◆ oral presentations?

◆ business meetings?

◆ social occasions?

◆ negotiation?

◆ business agreements?

◆ resolution of problems?

These and other expectations make up the business culture you must understand to work effectively abroad. To help you learn as much as possible about your target culture, we have assembled Internet addresses for the embassies in the United States of virtually all of the world's trading countries. In addition, we have provided Internet addresses for all U.S. embassies in trading countries abroad. As explained in Chapter 8, each of these U.S. embassies employs at least one foreign service officer with responsibility for facilitating trade. This person (paid for with your tax dollars) can be an extremely valuable resource in helping you understand the country's business culture, develop relationships with valuable business contacts, and make specific plans for fulfilling your business purposes in the country.

More general information on 30 primary trading countries can be found in Chapter 9.

Perhaps most valuable of all, however, are the comments contributed by cultural experts in the areas they represent (see Chapter 6, Intercultural Business Tips by Area Experts). A final list of companies, agencies, and organizations providing cross-cultural training completes what we have conceived of as a survival manual of sorts for the international businessperson.

THE BIG MISTAKE AND THE BIG WIN

American businesspeople who work abroad with little or no knowledge of local culture run the risk of making costly and embarrassing business mistakes. This danger is no less present for large companies than for individuals. However, knowledge of culture and local preferences can often turn a modest business exploration abroad into a gold mine.

The Big Mistake

Based on rosy statistics for household income in Germany and the Netherlands, executives at a major credit card company authorized a huge marketing campaign to put their card in the wallet or purse of every adult in those countries. After months of lackluster results, the company ruefully came to understand a cultural truth for Germany and the Netherlands: Buying on credit is not socially approved. The German word for debt *(schuld)* turns out to be the same word for guilt.

Could this result have been foreseen and prevented? Yes, but only with a combination of cultural humility ("What works in the United States won't work everywhere") and cultural knowledge ("The Germans can tell us what will work in Germany.") Consider several other big mistakes spawned by cultural ignorance:

Coca-Cola heavily advertised its two-liter bottle for the cost-conscious consumer in Spain until it discovered, to its chagrin, that the bottle would not fit in Spanish refrigerators.

Colgate launched a toothpaste in France under the product name "Cue" only to discover that *cue* is slang in French for "butt."

Buoyed by the success of its "no more cavities" campaign for Crest toothpaste, the company aired a similar marketing pitch throughout Mexico. Poor sales led the company to investigate cultural aspects of their message. It turns out that Mexicans, unlike U.S. consumers, don't choose toothpastes based on claims of decay prevention.

The Chinese government underwrote the manufacture and export of a line of men's underwear to the United States. It failed in large part due to the name chosen for the product line: "Pansy."

Kellogg's attempted to market its Bran Buds in Sweden, only to find that the label translated as "burned farmer" to Swedes.

Sunbeam spent heavily to introduce a curling iron to Germany under the name "Mist-Stick." The company learned too late that *mist* means "dung" or "manure" in German.

Procter & Gamble launched a successful series of international commercials for Camay facial soap. In the ads, men compliment women in a direct way on their appearance. The same ads failed miserably in Japan, where such direct compliments are considered unseemly.

Chevrolet's popular Nova automobile brought howls of laughter from locals when marketed under that name in South America, where *no va* means "won't go."

D.A. Ricks, in *Big Business Blunders,* recounts similar cultural disasters involving cars:

> *Fiera (a low-cost truck designed for developing countries) faced sales problems since* fiera *means "terrible, cruel, or ugly" in Spanish. The popular Ford car Comet had limited sales in Mexico, where it was named Caliente. The reason—* caliente *is slang for a streetwalker. The Pinto was briefly introduced in Brazil without a name change. Then it was discovered that* pinto *is slang for a "small male sex organ." The name was changed to Corcel, which means "horse."*

Esso gasoline experienced a similar problem in its attempts to enter the Japanese market, where its name (pronounced phonetically) means "stalled car."

Marketers don't have to go abroad to make cultural gaffes. *Advertising Age* gathered these memorable and expensive mistakes:

◆ When Frank Perdue's famous chicken slogan, "It Takes a Tough Man to Make a Tender Chicken," was translated directly into Spanish, it came out as "It Takes a Sexually Excited Man to Make a Chicken Affectionate."

◆ A candy manufacturer made reference to its "50 years" in the business on the wrappers of its candy bars. By neglecting to include the tilde mark over the "n" in the Spanish word for years, the manufacturer inadvertently told Spanish customers that the wrapper contained "50 anuses."

◆ Coors' beer slogan, "Get loose with Coors," came out in Spanish as "Get the runs with Coors."

Finally, colors, numbers, and symbols can have important cultural meaning, with implications for business. These examples have been collected by Del I. Hawkins, Roger J. Best, and Kenneth A. Coney in *Consumer Behavior* (1998).

> *A manufacturer of water-recreation products lost heavily in Malaysia because the company's predominant color, green, was associated with jungle and illness.*

> *A leading U.S. golf ball manufacturer was initially disappointed in its attempts to penetrate the Japanese market. Its mistake was packaging its golf balls in sets of four. Four is a symbol of death in Japanese.*

> *Pepsi-Cola lost its dominant market share in Southeast Asia to Coke when it changed the color of its coolers and vending equipment from deep "regal" blue to light "ice" blue. Light blue is associated with death and mourning in Southeast Asia.*

Most Chinese business travelers were shocked during the inauguration of United's concierge services for first-class passengers on its Pacific Rim routes. To mark the occasion, each concierge was proudly wearing a white carnation—an Asian symbol of death.

AT&T had to change its "thumbs-up" ads in Russia and Poland where showing the palm of the hand in this manner has an offensive meaning.

The Big Win

On the positive side, many American companies have used cultural knowledge to achieve remarkable business success abroad. McDonald's, for example, has dropped entirely its previous program of having one menu for the globe. It now offers fried eggs with its burgers in Japan, pork burgers with sweet barbecue sauce in Thailand, and the Maharaja Mac for non-beef-eating Hindus in India—"two all-mutton patties, special sauce, lettuce, cheese, pickles, onions on a sesame-seed bun."

General Foods took seriously their research in France that showed little consumption of orange juice for breakfast in that country. The company's Tang product is now marketed as a refreshment drink for any time during the day or night in the French market.

In the Middle East, many companies have tried to be first to market because of a curious, and potentially profitable, cultural trait. Once a particular product is accepted, consumers in the Middle East tend to call all similar products by the name of the originally purchased product. For example, all sports shoes are called Nikes, all detergents Tide, all vacuum cleaners Hoovers, and so forth.

Finally, before spreading its "Enjoy Coca-Cola" slogan around the world, the company investigated possible misinterpretations of the verb *enjoy*. It discovered that *enjoy* could not be separated from sensual connotations in several languages. In Russian, for example, the phrase "Enjoy Coca-Cola" would be understood, disastrously, as "Get Aroused with Coca-Cola." The company altered its logo to "Drink Coca-Cola" where necessary, and altered its "the real thing" slogan in Japan and elsewhere to the equivalent of "I feel Coke" (an expression, interestingly, that would not work at all in American English).

When its focus groups in Japan showed that Japanese women felt guilty for microwaving frozen vegetables instead of preparing them in traditional ways, Pillsbury revised its Green Giant frozen vegetable ads to emphasize the product's nutrition and convenience for "modern cooking." Apparently Japanese women were persuaded: sales jumped 50 percent.

American companies have increasingly devoted resources to achieve "the big win" when doing business abroad. Exxon, General Motors, and Procter & Gamble, among others, have recently spent $500,000 or more on cultural training programs for their employees.

Chapter 2

Windows to Other Cultures— and Your Own

GLOBAL BUSINESS

Let's not make the mistake of thinking about intercultural communication as a business phenomenon of the late twentieth century. In fact, people of different cultures have been communicating with one another about business matters for 5,000 years or more. However, the beginning of the twenty-first century has brought dramatic changes in the ease, frequency, and necessity for intercultural business relations. These changes are due primarily to improvements and innovations in electronic communications: the Internet, e-mail, fax, TV, radio, and teleconferencing help international banks and corporations carry on global business affairs. As a result, the car you drive probably contains parts from several nations. Your computer may contain chips and other components from a half dozen countries or more.

With the advent of Euro currency throughout European Union countries, formerly adversarial cultures are putting aside historical prejudices for the sake of advantageous business and social relations. A related development fostering peaceful interactions is the increasing presence of one country's business ventures on the soil of another country. Japanese, Korean, German, and Swedish automobile manufacturers have all opened manufacturing plants and assembly facilities in the United States. At the same time, U.S. business icons such as Ford and Coke are powerful and popular business names around the world. An increasing percentage of U.S. real estate is owned by foreign investors. Our television shows and recorded music is in many cases owned by foreign companies. Even the Seattle Mariners baseball team is partially owned by the Japanese game giant, Nintendo.

SHARED INFORMATION = SHARED CULTURE

What makes these sorts of international business relationships possible? Developed countries can now share information almost instantaneously. The globe has become a village, and like a village, its citizens can communicate with one another quickly and inexpensively. But for all our technological advances in communication, we still have miles to go before we resolve cultural barriers to doing business abroad.

In short, we may share much of the same information and technology with other nations, but we do not share detailed knowledge of one another's cultures. Werner Krause in Frankfurt and Togo Nagasone in Japan may share the same knowledge of Java computer programming as their Silicon Valley counterpart, Emily Westin, but they don't share the same cultural expectations, assumptions, and intentions. Their financial, religious, political, and other values are different.

Unlike rapid changes in chip technologies, cultures based on thousands of years of development are slow to change. For the foreseeable future, we can expect cultural barriers to pose a major challenge to companies and individuals seeking to do business outside their own borders. Those who take these barriers seriously and attempt to overcome them will reap significant business advantage abroad.

Managers who travel to foreign countries to do business know that they will encounter misunderstandings, even mysteries, in their efforts to communicate with coworkers and clients abroad. Being alert to those interpersonal obstacles can make or break a business transaction. Successful individuals, whether in business, industry, government, or science, know that in their relations with other cultures:

◆ There are no specific values or behaviors that are universally "right."

◆ They must be flexible and accepting of differences in values, beliefs, standards, and mores.

◆ They must be sensitive to verbal nuances and nonverbal signals.

◆ Knowledge of religious, cultural, business, and social practices of other cultures is a necessity.

◆ Within a foreign culture many different values and preferences may coexist.

DIFFERING PERCEPTIONS OF SPACE

Animals guard their territory by instinct. A similar sense of territoriality exists in nations, cultures, regions, cities, and even homes. To protect and define our territory we put up flags, fences, rows of bushes, signs, border markings, and so forth. How often have you seen a businessperson walk into a meeting room (or a student walk into a classroom), select a seat, then occupy it for every meeting or class in that room? Interestingly, no other person will tend to take that seat. It is already taken as territory.

Societal norms govern this sense of territory. Primary territories include items such as your bed, toothbrush, or comb—those items that are indisputably personal, private, and yours. Secondary territories include your chair at the dinner table and your desk at the office. Public territories are places such as the library, parking lot, beach, or picnic area. You claim space in such public territories by placing your books or jacket on the table in the library, unrolling your blanket on the beach, painting your name or title on a parking space, or placing your food on a picnic table. You establish personal space, a boundary of comfort around you that expands or contracts depending on the circumstances and cultural norms. In the United States, personal space for ordinary business conversation tends to be 3 to 5 feet. Intimate or highly sensitive communication tends to happen with 18 inches to 3 feet between the parties. That latter distance is typical of everyday personal space throughout Latin America.

If you do business with people from Mexico or Italy, you may notice that they tend to occupy more of your personal space than would someone from Germany or Scandinavia. Perhaps you have personally been involved, either within the United States or abroad, with an Italian or Mexican friend who is speaking with great excitement. He may be advancing, you may be retreating, and you both are puzzled. "Why is he moving into my space?" you wonder. "Why is he backing away when I address him? Does he disagree?" the puzzled friend ponders.

Space is also portioned out differently in businesses from culture to culture. Look at the president of a U.S. corporation as he or she sits in splendid isolation in a large office on the top floor with corner windows. By contrast, Japanese or Middle Eastern managing directors tend to sit among their subordinates so they can see all activities and be seen as a role model. Or consider the Japanese homeowner who often prefers a small living space that is well proportioned and includes only the items necessary for daily use. How different from suburban U.S. homeowners who measure their dwellings in thousands of square feet and fill them to overflowing with furnishings, exercise equipment, electronics, cooking appliances, spas, toys, and all manner of other consumer items.

The point here is not only that our preferred uses of space differ from culture to culture, but also that we are uncomfortable when those preferences are violated. Think of how individuals feel and relate when in a crowded elevator as opposed to an elevator containing only three or four people. Consider how crowd density in a prison yard (or, for that matter, a rock concert or sporting event) may encourage and permit panic and violence. Ignoring another culture's sense of space may invite thoughts and feelings that work against smooth business dealings.

DIFFERING PERCEPTIONS OF TIME

Cultures observe and experience time differently. In the United States, we tend to view time as a river forever moving on at constant pace. Because it always seems to be moving away from us, we are typically eager to save time, buy time, make time, spend time, or invest time. Not to do so in American business would be to waste time. We may become irritated when foreign business associates do not observe time commitments the way we do.

The U.S. businessperson dealing with someone whose cultural orientation is different must be aware of the possibility that this person may view time in quite different ways. The New York executive kept waiting 20 minutes past an appointment time with a foreign visitor should not automatically interpret the wait as a personal insult or a sign of the visitor's lack of professionalism. In that person's cultural view, a specific time on the clock may matter far less than clothes worn to the occasion, a gift brought out of respect, or the selection of a meeting place.

One business consultant gives this advice to Americans doing business abroad: "In many countries we are seen to be in a rush; in other words, unfriendly, arrogant, and untrustworthy. Almost everywhere, we must learn to wait patiently and never to push for deadlines. Count on things taking a long time, the definition of 'a long time' being at least twice as long as you would imagine."

DIFFERING VIEWS OF MATERIAL ITEMS

In the consuming culture of the United States, many individuals highly prize such items as expensive cars, furnishings, clothes, and homes. It may come as something of a surprise to realize that these items do not necessarily signal status, wisdom, or honorability for other cultures. The U.S. perception that "big is better" (whether in diamonds, houses, or office space) may seem not only quaint but mildly ridiculous to some Asian cultures, where beauty and proportion matter more than gross size: a bonsai tree, a meticulously tended garden, a carved netsuke, or intricately worked piece of jade.

DIFFERING VIEWS OF BUSINESS FRIENDSHIPS

Friendships are formed and maintained differently from culture to culture. Most businesspeople in the United States travel often in their work, and perhaps relocate every few years. They usually make business friendships quickly and easily wherever they go. New neighbors, church or synagogue members, and work associates almost immediately become "Mike" or "Melissa." But when U.S. businesspeople attempt or expect the same quick approach to friendship when working abroad, they often encounter stubborn and disappointing barriers to their efforts. Work associates in Europe and Asia may expect to be addressed by their formal last names for years before more informal relations are established. They may address you as "Mr." or "Ms." during this long period. They may have no thought of inviting you to their homes, and may feel awkward responding to an invitation to visit yours. In short, friendships develop slowly and carefully in many cultures. Even next-door neighbors in England or Germany may maintain for decades what seem to be icily formal relations to U.S. observers. Why not have a block party with beer and a barbecue? That's just not the culture, comes the response.

Foreign reliance upon lasting friendships is often a matter of business necessity. In Brazil and much of Latin America, for example, businesspeople despair of using their legal system to resolve business conflicts and problems. Instead of negotiating a contract (the American way) these businesspeople attempt to negotiate a lasting relationship in which sincerity, loyalty, and mutual compromises are key features. A similar approach is common in Japan and China.

AGREEMENTS
To a U.S. businessperson, an agreement completed with a signed contract is almost sacred. To break the contract means to be legally liable, not to mention the damage to one's integrity and reputation.

In the Middle East, however, a contract may be viewed somewhat suspiciously as "just a piece of paper" that can be undone as easily as the paper can be destroyed. The true agreement for these cultures may be constituted by a handshake between the parties after deliberate and thorough discussions over many cups of coffee. For some Arab business leaders, the presentation of a formalized contract for signatures may be taken as an affront and lack of trust. Throughout the countries of the former Soviet Union and in Greece, the signing of a contract (no matter what the contract language) is taken as the opening gambit in a give-and-take of business terms that continues throughout the business relationship.

Similarly in China, the understandings and mutual respect earned through many long conversations among the principals, often over meals, are far more influential in assuring compliance to business terms than a paper contract. Many U.S. construction firms that have embarked on major projects abroad have found that their foreign contractual partners look upon their carefully worded, legally reviewed contracts as just the beginning of negotiations, not the end.

ETHICS

The ethical standards and practices of one culture may seem repugnant to or may be patently illegal in another culture. For example, under-the-table payment to an individual or group to secure a contract would be termed a bribe in the United States. In many other cultures, such a monetary gesture is not illegal at all and is viewed as a form of commission for services rendered. Certain actions or comments in a U.S. office may be called "sexual harrassment" and are both unethical and illegal. In some Mediterranean offices, however, the same interactions may not be taken seriously at all.

DIFFERING VIEWS ON EATING CUSTOMS

Where, when, how, and with whom one dines carry vastly different messages and implications for different cultures. Who is served first, the men or women at the table? The young or the old? The host or those being hosted? Are women allowed to be present at an important meal? Is liquor expected at the meal or completely taboo? Are you expected to match your host toast for toast? To drink everything in your glass? Can you decline drinking entirely? Do you pass or reach for food? Does it matter whether you use your right or left hand in touching food (yes, in many Middle Eastern nations, where the left hand is considered unclean.) Do you participate in or remain silent during prayers at meals?

DIFFERING VIEWS ON MALE-FEMALE RELATIONS

What some cultures perceive as the natural and historical subordination of women to men strikes many Americans as unfortunate and unjust. The ethical and political issues involved come to a head when a U.S. businesswoman faces hard choices: Will she be effective in doing business in cultures that suppress women? Can she do so in good conscience?

The answers to these difficult questions are deeply personal and situational. But three trends have emerged in recent years:

1. Businesswomen are visiting sexually hostile cultures in increasing numbers. They are often accorded respect and a range of latitude not given to native women in those cultures.

2. When businesswomen anticipate problems due to sexual assumptions, they can prepare in advance by establishing their professional status with their foreign clients through correspondence, telephone conversation, and mutual acquaintances.

3. Women sometimes make initial business contacts in such cultures in the company of male colleagues, who then withdraw as the business relationship develops.

A favorite tenet of cultural relativism is that mores and customs are neither right nor wrong, just different. But in the case of sexual discrimination (or racial or ethic discrimination), cultures, like individuals, can simply be wrongheaded. Attitudes change, however, as women assert themselves as professionals equally capable with men to do business. Attitudes also change as economically disadvantaged cultures observe that wealthy trading cultures respect women.

MISCELLANEOUS CULTURAL CONTRASTS

There are many other areas where perceptions differ from one culture to another. An American man who brings his Berlin dinner hostess red roses (signifying romantic love) would cause more than a moment of discomfort. And white flowers (signifying mourning) would be equally inappropriate for a Belgian hostess.

Different cultures view odors differently. In the United States, people spend millions of dollars annually on deodorants and mouthwashes designed to eliminate or mask body odors. In contrast, Arabs may breathe in each other's faces while speaking. Not to do so is to "deny one's breath" and is considered a grave insult. Eskimo, Maori, Samoans, and Philippine Islanders may rub noses or inhale as they place their nose against the cheeks of others. Dominant scents or odors are often associated with particular cultures, usually stemming from diet. Depending on the culture, the heavy odor of garlic, the haze of cigarette smoke, or the scent of whisky on the breath may be olfactory barriers that the American manager may have to accept and overcome in doing business abroad.

Paralanguage

Cultural differences also appear in paralanguage—that is, a behavior that interrupts, accompanies, or takes the place of speech. It may be a gesture, a movement of a hand, eyebrow, or face, or posture. It may be a sound such as a grunt, whistle, or sigh. Paralanguage can even include a short or extended silence. The physician's sound of "ummm" while staring at the lab or x-ray report and the inward gasp of air as someone reads bad or good news in a letter are examples of paralanguage that communicate a message.

We must be careful not to impose American paralanguage signals on other cultures. The long silence on the part of Japanese managers during a negotiation is probably not a sign of disapproval or reluctance. Instead, they remain silent for a prolonged period to show that they respect the offer under consideration and desire to examine it thoroughly. The frequent nod of the head given by such Japanese businesspeople does not mean that they agree with what you are saying, merely that they are understanding you. Similarly, their averted eyes is not a signal of discomfort in your presence so much as a customary gesture of respect.

Typical U.S. attitudes toward touching are vastly different from that of many other cultures in the world. It is not unusual in Europe or the Middle East to see two men or two women walking together with hands clasped or even encircling a shoulder or waist. Such a sight remains as unusual here as seeing two men greet each other with a kiss on one cheek or both—a relatively common sight in many other cultures.

Discussion between a manager and a subordinate in the United States may occur with each in a very relaxed posture. They might be drinking coffee. If the manager is a man (or, for that matter, a women in a pantsuit), a foot may be casually hooked over an empty chair or planted on a nearby table top. Not so in the Middle East where crossed legs or facing the soles of one's shoes toward another individual is a sign of rudeness. In many cultures, certainly throughout Asia and Europe, the subordinate is expected to be virtually "at attention" when in conference with a superior. For example, keeping your hands in your pockets when addressing your German or Austrian boss is just not done.

In the United States we are sometimes concerned when the other person does not look us in the eye or seems otherwise visually evasive. We suspect discomfort on the person's part, and perhaps a lack of honesty or integrity. In Japan, a businessperson may interpret a lack of respect if another individual does look directly eye-to-eye. Such eye contact may well signal defiance, hostility, or impertinence.

Professional Status

U.S. businesspeople have no hesitancy, when asked, to list our accomplishments and other status markers. In much of Asia such a presentation would seem out of place and in bad taste. One's *meishi* or presentation of professional status is accomplished in the ritual of presenting one's business card (usually with accompanying translation on the reverse side of the card for the convenience of the person receiving the card). When accepting a business card, the person is expected in Asian cultures to pay attention to it for a few moments, to comment appropriately on the person's status, to thank the person for offering the card, and to give a card in response. For both parties, the presentation of the card is usually made with a slight bow, and always with both hands holding the card.

It would be culturally unwise for an American manager to single out one Chinese, Korean, or Japanese employee in the presence of his or her coworkers for extended praise. While this is common practice in the United States, such spotlighting of the individual would be embarrassing for all concerned in many Asian business cultures. "The nail that protrudes must be knocked down," goes the Japanese saying.

Finally, a myriad of etiquette differences separate cultures, and consequently separate us somewhat as individuals in those cultures. Does one bring a gift, for example, to a business meeting? Probably not in Russia, Taiwan, or Germany, but emphatically yes in Japan. And how should gifts be presented? Privately in China, but in front of others throughout Arab countries. What should the gift be? A tasteful item of craft or artistry from your own culture would be appropriate throughout Asia. Personal gifts (e.g., jewelry) for the wives of foreign business associates would be considered out of bounds throughout Latin America and much of Europe. Some gifts have the wrong symbolic import: cutlery, for example, is entirely the wrong gift in Germany, Taiwan, and Russia.

Language

Fortunately for most monolingual American businesspeople, trading nations around the world are moving toward making English the international language of business. But American English is often not the same as British English, as many U.S. businesspeople have experienced to their dismay. *Satisfactory* in American English means *minimally acceptable,* but to the British can be interpreted from *acceptable* to *excellent.* An apartment is a *flat;* a druggist is a *chemist;* and a period at the end of a sentence is a *full-stop.*

Add to these problems with varieties of English the larger semantic difficulties involved in translation from one language to another. As illustrated at the beginning of this book, some of these language misunderstandings are downright humorous (so long as we are not the one's who suffer the loss of money and face associated with them). A group of Hispanic ad agencies in Los Angeles have formed an organization called Merito: the Society for Excellence in

Hispanic Advertising. The organization has as its mission the "elimination of misunderstandings, bad translations, and bad advertising by nonHispanics to the Hispanic market." The group cites examples such as the slogan used by Braniff Airline: "travel on leather." The Spanish word for leather (cuero) also means *naked*— with the resulting message, *travel naked.*

Examples abound from other cultures as well. "Come alive with Pepsi" was inadvertently translated into German as "Come out of the grave with Pepsi." In Asia, "Body by Fisher" stamped on U.S.-exported autos was read as "Corpse by Fisher." Common U.S. sayings such as "the spirit is willing but the flesh is weak" became in Russian "the ghost is ready but the meat is rotten."

These are extreme examples, of course, but they point up the care American managers must take in relying on translation to communicate their key messages.

Equal care must be taken with colors, numbers, and other symbols. Here is one summary of approximate cultural differences for these aspects of intercultural communication:

White	*Symbol for mourning or death in the Far East; purity in the United States.*
Purple	*Associated with death in many Latin American countries.*
Blue	*Connotation of femininity in Holland; masculinity in Sweden.*
Red	*Unlucky or negative in Chad, Nigeria, Germany; positive in Denmark, Rumania, Argentina. Brides wear red in China, but it is a masculine color in the United Kingdom and France.*
Yellow flowers	*Sign of death in Mexico; infidelity in France.*

White lilies	*Suggestion of death in England.*
7	*Unlucky number in Ghana, Kenya, Singapore; lucky in Morocco, India, Czechoslovakia, Nicaragua, United States.*
Triangle	*Negative in Hong Kong, Korea, Taiwan; positive in Colombia.*
Owl	*Wisdom in the United States; bad luck in India.*
Deer	*Speed, grace in the United States; homosexuality in Brazil.*

DIFFERENCES IN BUSINESS MANNERISMS AND EXPECTATIONS

Joking among strangers or new acquaintances makes Germans ill at ease. At meetings or in presentations, while an American or Briton might feel obliged to crack a joke or two, or an Italian or French person indulges in witticism, a German will often remain consistently serious, neither using humor nor responding to it. Humor, in short, is an expected icebreaker for many cultures; but for others it is both unexpected and inappropriate.

The most marked difference between business communications in Korea and the United States is the difference between American objectivity and Korean subjectivity. For businesspeople in the United States, relationships and personal feelings (both positive and negative) are to be set aside in favor of impartial and dispassionate logic. For Koreans, sincerity and commitment to individuals are the basis for business dealings. Business is transacted by two people, not by the firms they represent.

Business meetings in Italy are usually unstructured and informal. They do not follow preestablished agendas and participants may (and do!) come and go as the meeting progresses. Anyone may speak at any time, and eloquence, not status, is the key to earning an audience. Decisions implemented later by the company may have no bearing at all on those made in the meeting.

In Vietnam, the boss is the boss—anytime, anywhere. In the United States, an executive away from the office can relax and pursue leisure in any way he or she chooses. In Vietnam, leisure must be pursued according to one's station in business and in life generally. Executives in Vietnam would never eat in simple, small restaurants because the food is good; they must go only to first-rate, elegant restaurants to maintain image and reputation (their own and their company's).

Latin Americans tend to view all of life holistically, and this perspective applies to business relations as well. Whereas a good conversation between U.S. businesspeople is one that is focused, task-oriented, and concise, one between Latin Americans is more likely to touch on various topics, to consider each subject from all possible dimensions, and to move only indirectly toward a conclusion.

As these illustrations demonstrate, beliefs, value systems, and communications vary widely for business purposes around the world. So how are people working in the global marketplace to communicate effectively wherever they go? How does one know, from Tokyo to Beijing to Rome, what is appropriate or not, what behavior will be understood as intended and what could cause a cross-cultural relationship to collapse? Is it necessary to become intimate with every culture in which a firm seeks to do business?

John Mole, an English author and consultant, writes in his book, *When in Rome...A Business Guide to Cultures and Customers in Europe*, that although the more you know about each country the better, you can use a simple system to make general assumptions about the differences in doing business in different nations. His work around the world for Mellon Bank—in the United States, Africa, the Middle East, and Europe—convinced him that there are two major factors in determining how people interact and in what ways interactions differ from company to company and culture to culture. The first factor is a set of beliefs about organization and the place of people within it: the ways work is organized, forecasting and planning processes, the techniques of gathering and disseminating information, and the measurement of results. The second factor is a set of beliefs about leadership; these beliefs involve the bases of authority, the ownership of power, and the process of decision making.

The organization dimension takes shape in a firm based on the extent to which the firm believes that a rational system should be imposed on human endeavor. Depending on how much systems are valued, the organization may range in type from loose and informal to highly structured and bureaucratic. Mole uses the terms organic/systematic to denote this range.

The leadership dimension takes shape based on the extent to which a firm thinks that power is best used through groups or individuals. The forms of leadership may cover the spectrum from centralized and authoritarian to team-based and egalitarian. Mole uses the terms group/individualistic to denote this range.

With the broad dimensions of organization and leadership, Mole plots the business cultures of various nations. The "Mole Map" shows nine countries. Mole notes that these are generalizations about business organizations and leadership methods, and that within national cultures and across industries similar differences can also be plotted.

The placement of the United States in the upper-right quadrant—high on organizational structure and high on individualistic leadership compared with everyone else—runs counter to the way we tend to view ourselves. While informality and a casual approach are hallmarks of the U.S. communication style and lifestyle, when it comes to business we more closely resemble the rigid hierarchy and authoritarianism of, say, the military than does any other nation. If the first impression we have of an international firm is that its organization is chaotic and its leadership capricious, we must at the same time bear in mind that to them we may appear impenetrably bureaucratic, rigidly controlled, and almost robotic in our limited range of options as businesspeople.

Figure 2-1

THE ORGANIZATION DIMENSION

Organic		*Systematic*
Plans are based on hunches, intuition, and experience and are expressed in words.	Forecasting	Plans are based on analysis and expressed in numbers.
Decisions evolve and are based on judgment.	Decision Making	Decisions are made and are based on fact.
Authority is based on trust; who you know matters most; accountability is vague.	Supervision	Authority is based on competence; accountability is clear.
Errors are blamed on people and lead to recrimination; criticism is personal.	Control	Errors are blamed on the system and lead to improvement; criticism is objective.
Communication is informal and people read between the lines (what does it mean?).	Communication	Communication goes through official channels and people read what is printed (what does it say?).
The right connections earn promotion; success depends on luck, and educational qualifications indicate breeding.	Reward	Competence earns promotion; success depends on skill; and educational qualifications indicate professionalism.
People strive for esteem, take pride in their status, and compete by outmaneuvering.	Motivation	People strive for achievement, take pride in professionalism, and compete by outperforming.
Rules are to be circumvented; informal associations and alliances are the real basis of the organization.	Style	Rules are to be obeyed; the organization chart shows reality.

THE LEADERSHIP DIMENSION

Group		*Individualistic*
Planning is done by those responsible; everyone should know what the strategy is.	Forecasting	Planning is done by top management; only a few need to know the strategy.
Groups make decisions; consensus is paramount; everybody's opinion accounts for something.	Decision Making	Individuals make decisions; decisiveness is paramount; a superior's view always outweighs a subordinate's.
Authority must be constantly earned; leaders stay close to their followers and embody the will of the group.	Supervision	Authority must be demonstrated; leaders keep their distance and impose their will on the group.
Quality is a mutual concern and groups are accountable.	Control	Quality has to be enforced and individuals are accountable.
Communication moves in all directions; meetings are for information sharing and people should be good listeners.	Communication	Communication is downward; meetings are for briefing and people should be good communicators.
Teams strive for goals and are rewarded.	Reward	Individuals strive for achievement and are rewarded.
People work for the team, are self-motivated, and want harmony to predominate.	Motivation	People work for themselves, have to be directed, and thrive on competition.
Hierarchy, status, and subtleties are a convenience and modesty is prized.	Style	Hierarchy is essential and people should be assertive and confident.

U.S. VALUES

Ironically, an American just returning from a two-week trip to France may find it easier to answer the question, "What do the French value?" than the question, "What do Americans value?" The differences of viewpoint and approach to life and business seem clear to us after only a short exposure to another culture whereas our own cultural experience—in effect, the cultural air we breathe—remains foggy and undefined.

By taking time to look squarely at our own cultural assumptions and beliefs, we equip ourselves to find points of similarity and difference with other cultures. We may also become more humble and less apt to claim cultural superiority; a close look at dominant U.S. values at least raises the question of their ethical basis. In the following list, some of the suggested values may not be yours. Judge, however, whether you believe these values to be generally shared by American culture.

PERSONAL CONTROL OVER THE ENVIRONMENT

In the United States, people consider it normal and proper that human beings control nature. That may mean changing the size of a mountain, the location of a lake, the direction or even the existence of a river, and perhaps even the genetic structure of a living organism. Most of the world's population think that such changes are fraught with danger. Fate, they believe, plays a powerful role in human life. Natural structures and forces are the face of fate—immutable, unyielding, and not to be manipulated by mere humans. This rubric applies in many cultures to notions of cleanliness, beyond minimal standards. To be overly concerned about cleanliness may seem unnatural to many cultures—in effect, a disturbance of the natural order of things.

CHANGE

People in the United States usually feel change is a good thing—something that signals progress and brings renewed interest and excitement to living. Change is associated with development, growth, and advancement. Older cultures, however, often view change as disruptive and destructive. The established order, for all its flaws, is usually preferable in these cultures to the unknown and unpredictable results of new beginnings, revolutions, and social experiments.

CONTROL OF TIME

Time exerts both control and pressure on people in the United States. Time here is valuable and highly prized. Not to observe time commitments is interpreted as a sign of discourtesy to others, lack of ambition, and general slovenliness. Other cultures worry no more about time than fish apparently worry about the water in which they swim. Time is simply "there"—a medium in which people pursue their activities and relationships.

EQUALITY

By our Constitution and tradition, we view individuals as created equal. We value equality as an important civic and social goal. But in most of the world, rank, status, and authority are viewed as part and parcel of everyday life, including business life. To many individuals in other cultures, knowing who they are and where they fit in the various strata of their society offers a sense of security. In such cultures, the king would not choose to be a pauper, and the pauper would not choose to be a king.

INDIVIDUALISM AND PRIVACY

People in the United States feel strongly that they are individuals who deserve and expect fair treatment for their unique viewpoints and qualities. In other cultures, especially where space is at a premium in homes, offices, and workplaces, the concept of individualism is of less importance. One's membership in the group and one's flexibility in meeting group goals take precedence.

SELF-HELP

Americans take pride in "making it" on their own. If we accept inherited wealth, we downplay it and focus instead on our efforts to make our own contribution to our welfare. The same is not true of many other cultures, where the self-made man or woman may be given much less respect than the person endowed with wealth or position by birthright or class.

COMPETITION AND FREE ENTERPRISE

Americans value competition and stress it in the classroom, on the sports field, and in the boardroom. But in societies that value cooperation, the intense competitiveness of the United States is not easy to comprehend. "Getting ahead" for the individual is seen as essentially antisocial in nature and destructive of larger social goals.

FUTURE ORIENTATION

People in the United States constantly work, plan, and strive for a better future. We set long- and short-term goals; we devise strategies to improve the future whether they are economic, social, athletic, or medical. But much of the world may perceive an attempt to alter the future as futile and perhaps even sinful. "What will be, will be" goes the refrain. In some cultures, the character of a person is shown more in the ability to accept what the future brings rather than in trying to influence the future.

ACTION AND WORK VALUES

Americans work long and hard. Their workdays are planned, with work activities scheduled weeks or months in advance. We become so involved in and defined by work activities that we become workaholics. Many cultures consider such monomaniacal focus on work both inhuman and destructive. Meditation, recreation, and human relations are valued above the additional wealth that could be achieved by a heavier workload.

DIRECTNESS, OPENNESS, AND HONESTY

People from other countries often look upon us as being blunt, perhaps even unfeeling. But people in the United States may pride themselves on "telling it like it is." This direct approach is difficult to understand for an individual who comes from a society where saving face is important and where communicating unpopular judgments or information may be dangerous. We may lose interest in people—wimps—who hint at what they intend or how they feel rather than stating the situation directly. By contrast, members of other cultures often lose trust in us because of our directness.

PRACTICALITY AND EFFICIENCY

People in the United States tend to evaluate situations with such questions as "Will it pay off?" and "Have we planned correctly?" Other cultures are less concerned with practicality and efficiency, concentrating instead on philosophic ends ("Is it right?"), aesthetic values ("Is it beautiful?"), or social goals ("Will it advance the welfare of the people?").

MATERIALISM

Most people in other cultures perceive Americans as being more materialistic than we perceive ourselves. We look upon our cars, appliances, homes, TV's, computers, and other material items as our just rewards for hard work. In contrast, many others see us as partners in a demented love affair with the things of this world, as if amassing an ever-growing collection of such material items would guarantee contentment and enlightenment.

Chapter 3

Writing, Speaking, and Listening in Other Cultures

CORRESPONDENCE

Most cultures are more formal than the United States in both writing and speaking. U.S. businesspeople should use titles when addressing their counterparts in the rest of the world. Unless you have a longstanding relationship with someone abroad and have

already used his or her first name in casual conversation, always use a surname and title. (A German professional may even be addressed as Herr Dr. Professor—three titles!)

Opening paragraphs of a letter in international correspondence are usually formal or introductory. Brief comments on the weather, a previous trip or association, or a noncontroversial international event or incident are quite appropriate as icebreakers. Giving best wishes for the time of year (the New Year in Asia, for example) or season is also common and welcomed. Sensitive factors such as late payments, behavior of representatives, and errors or delays in shipping should be handled with great delicacy and tact.

Business documents in various countries differ not only in form but also in pattern of organization, tone, and level of detail. German documents, for example, are terse and heavily detailed, while Latin American documents emphasize a polite, refined style and generalized concepts. Reports for Japanese associates must be prepared with formal, honorific openings. Omit casual analogies and other non-business-related information from the reports and proposals sent to British colleagues.

Even when you try to follow the style and tone of the documents written by native businesspeople in Latin America, Asia, and Europe, your Americanness will still show. Some of that is certainly acceptable. Intercultural readers, whether located inside the United States or abroad, expect American communications to show the features of American document conventions.

Nonetheless, shrewd intercultural communicators still try hard to bend their writing habits and assumptions toward the communication needs and expectations of their readers. As a case in point, many European cultures expect significant business correspondence to end with two signatures—the signatures of both the letter

テンポラリーワーカーズ株式会社　御中　　　　　　1989年10月 2日

　　　　　　　　　　　　　　　　　　　　　五菱商事株式会社

　　　　　　　　　　　　　　　　　　　　　取締役人事部長

　　　　　　　　　　　　　　　　　　　　　山田　太郎

　　　　　　　　　　業務秘書派遣依頼の件

拝啓、

　　貴社益々御隆昌の段お慶び申し上げます。また、平素より格別のお引き立ての程誠に有

難く存じます。

　　扱て、頭書の件に関し、弊社に於きましては、今般米国GU社と合弁企業を設立する運

びとなり、新会社の為の業務秘書を二名新規募集致します。就きましては、貴社の幅広い

人材の中から、下記条件に適合する候補者を弊社人事第一課宛御推薦戴ければ幸いです。

貴社より御推薦戴きました候補者につきまして、追って面談日時等を取り決めさせていた

だきたく存じます。

　　お忙しい中とは存じますが、本件に就いての御検討を宜しくお願い申し上げます。

　　　　　　　　　　　　　　　　　　　　　　　　　　　敬具

　　　　　　　　　　　　　記

　　　弊社希望条件　1. 英語能力（英検二級以上）

　　　　　　　　　　　2. 和文ワードプロセサー（二級以上）

　　　　　　　　　　　3. コンピュータ経験有り

　　　　　　　　　　　　　　　　　　　　　　　以上

Figure 3-1

Messrs: Temporary Workers Corporation   October 2, 1998

                                           Five Diamond Corporation
                                           Director, General Manager
                                           Taro Yamada

                                                      (official seal)

                    Subject: Secretary Recruiting

Dear Sir:
    It is our pleasure for serving you. I would like to take this opportunity to thank you for supporting our company for many years.

    *(Meantime,) We have finalized a plan to establish a joint-venture with GU Company, our American partner. And we have started looking for two secretaries for this project. Among your numerous capable candidates, we wish you can recommend two people to us with the undermentioned abilities. We will set up interviews with the appointed candidates immediately after receiving your recommendation.

    *(We guess that you are busy, however.) We will appreciate your reply as soon as possible.

                                                With our best regards.

                            Supplements
                        Requested Conditions
                1. Fluent English ability (above JST grade-2)
                2. Japanese wordprocessing ability (above grade-2)
                3. Experience of computers

            *Approximate equivalents for untranslatable Japanese phrases.

Figure 3-2

47

writer and his or her superior. Therefore, to get more positive reaction from a European reader, the American letter writer may decide to use two signatures.

An American writer may even have to learn when not to write at all. As reported in separate studies by Michael Yoshino and William Ouchi, Japanese companies don't use written communication for routine business matters as much as American companies do. If an American writer communicates solely by memo, a Japanese reader may tend to treat the message as being inappropriately serious or important—calling a meeting, for example, to discuss the implications of the memo. Instead, alternate channels of communication should be chosen: a conference telephone call, perhaps, or a face-to-face meeting in person or via teleconference with selected decision makers.

A final example involves the use of first names. In American correspondence, it is common after the first two or three business contacts to begin addressing the reader by his or her first name. This practice is generally taken in our culture to be a sign of friendliness and trust. In Germany, however, business readers look upon the use of first names (Dear Helmut) as a sign of inappropriate chumminess bordering on disrespect. For Germans, friendliness, trust, and respect in correspondence is demonstrated by the writer's willingness to use titles and surnames: Dear Director Schmidt.

Notice in the Japanese memo (Figure 3-1), written by a Mitsubishi manager, with accompanying translation (Figure 3-2), how the American "To/From/Subject/Date" material has been redistributed at the top of the memo page. An official seal—the personal trademark of a Japanese manager—appears beside the name. As with Japanese business tradition and Mitsubishi practice, this memo begins with standard language of respect. Following this traditional expression of respect and well-wishing, the memo turns to its specific business—in this case, the hiring of two secretaries. Note that the requested quali-fications of these secretaries are appended to the memo in the form of supplements, a common Japanese way of handling lists and details. The memo ends by turning again to traditional, expected language. No signature appears after the phrase, "with our best regards."

An American response to the Japanese manager's memo appears in Figure 3-3. The American memo endeavors to catch the form and spirit of the Japanese memo form without mimicking it in all details. The American writer would probably fail badly, for exam-ple, in trying to imitate all the nuances of the traditional Japanese beginning and ending. In this memo, the American writer begins rather formally, addresses the request in a general way, and high-lights details by a numbered list. But why go to the trouble to fol-low Japanese practice in these matters? A typical memo in the succinct, frank American style may have been misunderstood by the Japanese manager as an impatient, glib, or even mildly insult-ing response.

Five Diamond Corporation
Director, General Manager
Taro Yamada

October 3, 1998

Temporary Workers Corporation
Vice President
Richard Matthews

Subject: Your Request for Secretaries

Thank you for contacting Temporary Workers Corporation for your employment needs. We have certainly enjoyed being of service to you for the past four years.

After a careful review of sixteen highly skilled candidates, we have selected two secretaries to meet the needs you describe. Both are available at your convenience for an interview. We believe their considerable skills (listed below) will justify their employment.

We recognize that these are indeed busy times for you. However, we will be most pleased to hear from you as soon as possible to schedule interviews.

With sincere best wishes.

Supplements
Qualifications of Both Candidates

1. Grade 3 English ability in speaking and writing
2. Grade 3 Japanese wordprocessing ability
3. Experience with Japanese and American computer systems

Figure 3-3

In the Latin American memo and its English translation (Figures 3-4 and 3-5), note the distribution of the message on the page (somewhat lower than American practice); the convention of assigning numbers to memos; the use of the term "Antecedent"; the respectful tone, particularly in the memo opening; and letter-like conclusion. Figure 3-6 shows an American response in the style of a Chilean memo.

A Russian memo regarding personnel problems and its English translation are shown in Figures 3-7 and 3-8. Note the initial gesture of respect, followed by a straightforward statement of the problem. The problem is reinforced by lines that imply a state of near-desperation. The memo closes as it began, on a highly formal note. The writer signs his name in full. Figure 3-9 shows an American response in the form of a Russian memo.

A CULTURAL CASE STUDY: CHINA

Because Chinese cultural and business practices are less well known to most Americans than are those of Japan or Western trading nations, we include here an extended description of our experiences with a major retail arm of the Chinese government.

Geographically, culturally, and economically, China represents a huge footprint on the globe. At its present rate of economic growth, China may surpass the United State in gross national product (GNP) by the second decade of the new century. Even though much of its one billion people now live below the poverty level, the Chinese enjoy a vision of things to come. "One billion people—but 900,000,000 *business*people," goes the popular Chinese saying.

In preparation for writing this chapter on intercultural business opportunities, we visited China to meet with more than 200 business

/MEMORANDUM No. 532

Ant.: Su memorandum no. 228
de fecha 25.7.98.

Mat.:Solicitud de una
secretaria edicional.

Santiago, 12 de septiembre de 1998

DE: GERENTE DE FINANZAS

A: GERENTE GENERAL

De acuerdo a su memorandum de antecedente, me dirijo a usted con el objeto de solicitarle una secretaria adicional para nuestra gerencia. Como es de su conocimiento, nuestra unided ha tenido un gran crecimiento en los ultimos 5 meses. Se han contratado tres jóvenes profesionales y no se ha aumentado nuestra dotación de personal administrativo. En la actualidad contamos con tres secretarias, muy competentes, pero que no dan abasto con todo el trabajo requerido. Esto no nos permite alcanzar el rendimiento deseado.

La naturaleza de nuestras operaciones hace indispensable que la secretaria que se contrate tenga dominio del idioma inglés, tanto oral como escrito. Adicionalmente, debe estar familiarizada con el uso de procesadores de texto y de Lotus 1-2-3.

Agradezco de antemano su consideración.

Atentamente,

Juan González R.

Figure 3-4

MEMORANDUM No. 532

Antecedent: your memorandum
#228 of 07.25.98

Subject: request of an
additional secretary

Santiago, September 12, 1998

FROM: FINANCE MANAGER

TO: GENERAL MANAGER

Regarding your memorandum of antecedent, I am addressing you with the object of requesting an additional secretary for our department. As you know, our unit has had considerable growth during the last five months. Three young professionals have been recruited and the administrative staff has not increased. At present we have three very competent secretaries, but they are not able to do all the work required. This has not permitted us to obtain the desired performance.

The nature of our operations requires that the secretary who is hired has proficiency in oral and written English. In addition, she must be familiar with the use of word processors and Lotus 1-2-3.

Thank you in advance for your consideration.

Sincerely yours,

Juan González R.

Figure 3-5

Memorandum #541

Antecedent: Your memorandum #534

Sept. 12, 1998

Material: Response to your request for
an additional secretary

To: Finance Manager

From: General Manager

Regarding your request for additional secretarial support, I wish to suggest an alternate way of resolving the problem you describe. Instead of hiring an additional secretary, I propose that you send overflow typing and accounting work to the General Manager's secretarial pool. These employees are often seeking additional work and should be able to give you the support you require.

I have asked the Word-processing Supervisor to make specific arrangements with you for routing work expeditiously.

Thank you for bringing this problem to my attention and for your cooperation in trying out the solution I suggest.

Sincerely,

Helen Williams

Figure 3-6

Святослав Николаевич Кислородов
Заместитель директора по кадрам

Уважаемый Господин Кислородов,

У нас в отделении АСУ не хватает секретаршей.
Несколько дней уже у нас нет способности даже выполнять
все очередные документы. Что нам делать? Пожалуйста,
немедленно дайте нам разрешение добавить лишь одну
секретаршу.

С уважением,

Борис Иванович Боголюбимов

Figure 3-7

Svyatoslav Nikolayevich Kislorodov
Deputy to the Director for Personnel

Dear Mr. Kislorodov,

We do not have enough secretaries in our MIS department. For the last few days we have not even been able to fill out the regular documents. What are we to do? Please, immediately give us permission to add at least one more secretary.

Respectfully yours,

Boris Ivanovich Bogolyubimov

Figure 3-8

managers and leaders in several trading regions of that vast country. This narrative sums up what we learned about intercultural communication with businesspeople in China. We offer these comments and suggestions as guidelines for your communication with and, perhaps, travel to an emerging economic giant.

◆ *The Chinese (unlike the French, in some cases) appreciate your attempt to speak a bit of their language.* Understand, however, that the Chinese widely spoken in Hong Kong and the Economic Zone Territories is Cantonese. The Chinese spoken in Beijing and most of the rest of China is Mandarin. Strong feelings are attached in some regions to this language difference. Mandarin speakers in Beijing, for example, may not understand (or pretend not to understand) your tourist phrases spoken in Cantonese. Similarly, Cantonese speakers in Hong Kong may quickly "correct" your Mandarin attempts to their Cantonese equivalent.

9/2/98

Boris Ivanovich Bogolyubimov
Supervisor, MIS Department

Honored Comrade Bogolyubimov,

Supervisor Kislorodov has asked me to respond to your memorandum of Sept. 1, 1998. Like you, we feel the daily need for additional secretarial support. Our official documents are often prepared less quickly than we would wish. Such delays must be expected for the next several months until we receive final approval for Research Allocation Request #607.

I will look to you for patience and ingenuity in continuing to perform your duties admirably under the current conditions. I request that you send Mashinka to meet with Supervisor Kislorodov at 10 A.M., Sept. 15, 1998.

With great respect,

William Evans Phillips
American Liaison for MIS Research

Figure 3-9

◆ *Food and sociability are intimately linked with business discussions and decision making.* Your Chinese host will offer tea and probably a meal as part of your business visit. (When visiting the United States, your Chinese guest will expect the same from you.) Although topics of conversation at the table may touch on business matters, more often the Chinese prefer to use meal times as periods of relaxation—a chance to ask questions about your country, to talk about food, the weather, customs in different parts of China, family life (they will appreciate seeing pictures of your friends and family), and many other comfortable topics. Especially in your first meals together, the topics of politics and religion are generally out of bounds. Your questions in these areas will probably be greeted by a polite, ambiguous, and short answer.

◆ *At a formal meal with Chinese business hosts, you will probably be given a wrapped gift.* It is customary to thank your host and to set the gift aside for opening later. In response, you may present your host with a small, wrapped gift in return. (Your Chinese hosts will not expect such a gift, however; they know that gift-giving customs differ in the United States.) You need not bring a gift for each businessperson at the table. Presenting one gift to your primary host at the table is considered to be giving a gift to all. The most appreciated gifts are those that represent your country in some way or can be set on a shelf or mantle—a regional bowl, a decorative piece, and so forth. Less appropriate are items of personal jewelry or company products. (One U.S. automobile salesperson presented his Chinese host with a chromed carburetor from his company. It still sits on the host's desk as a standing joke.)

◆ *The Chinese believe deeply in the value of* guan xi *("relationship").* They want to know you deeply (your history, your motives, your personality, and especially your interaction with others) before committing to business relationships. This process of getting to know you takes time—and often many meals together. Be patient, self-disclosing, and gracious during what may seem to you to be a prolonged period of relationship-building.

◆ *Most successful contracts with the Chinese involve behind-the-contract components.* In a state-supervised economy, few Chinese businesspeople see direct personal results from their successful business relations with you. They typically do not receive commissions or other bonuses based on their performance (although this situation is changing, especially in the new Economic Zone Territories). As an incentive to accept your contract, Chinese businesspeople are quite receptive to "behind-the-contract" add-ons such as trips at your expense to visit your company in the United States, special equipment given to them as a marginal aspect of the contract, and other perks. Explicit bribes are both unwelcome and illegal in China.

◆ *Even after friendships have been established, the Chinese maintain a level of formality in address.* One story will make the point. After visiting and traveling with Ming Xuan Liu, our Chinese host, over a period years, he asked us "What shall I call you now that we are friends?" We responded, "Art and Gary." Then we asked in return (expecting his answer to be "Ming" or "Ming Xuan") what we should call him. He replied, without smiling, "Mr. Liu." The Mr. and Ms. forms of address are maintained as a sign of respect even in lifelong friendships (and, we are told, within many Chinese marriages!).

◆ *The Chinese want you to enjoy and approve of their culture and country; they are sensitive about discussions of poverty.* Much of China strikes the Western visitor as poor, dirty, and ugly. At the same time, the grandeur of Chinese culture, history, geography, monuments, and recent economic progress is undeniable. As a general rule, Chinese businesspeople will avoid conversations that delve too deeply into the Third World aspects of the country.

◆ *Finally, the Chinese are excellent negotiators by leaving many details of contracts and business arrangements unspecified.* Although no strict *quid pro quo* is intended by their hospitality and relationship building, the Chinese operate on the assumption that business friends go far beyond the letter of the law to make contracts work to mutual advantage. From a Western perspective, not a little guilt plays a part in this Chinese strategy. We may feel obligated to offer extra services and other accommodations to Chinese hosts who have been so gracious to us. Conversely, Chinese businesspeople often reject business deals that focus too closely on legal recourse, exact specifications of deliverables, and penalties for delays or other interruptions.

As one Chinese business student explained to us, "China is a land of people, not laws." In this brief phrase he was suggesting that the most successful business relationships between China and foreign business interests have been forged as much at the dining table as at the boardroom table. In dealing with a relationship-oriented society, communication skills could not be more valuable in achieving bottom line business results.

ASPECTS OF INTERCULTURAL LISTENING

Just as writing and speaking forms and approaches differ from culture to culture, so do listening habits and outward manifestations of attention. In Western cultures, intense listening is usually signalled by sustained eye contact given by the audience to the speaker along with responsive facial expressions (smiles, nods, and so forth). In many Asian cultures, however, the same degree of intense listening may be indicated by an averted gaze, with little animation of facial features. Western speakers new to such cultures must be careful not to judge the attention or interest level of an Asian audience by Western signs of listening.

In virtually all Western business environments, it would be considered impolite for an audience member to mill about, whisper to others, or leave the room entirely (except for emergencies) during a presentation. Not so in Japan and some other Asian business cultures, where it is commonplace for audience members in a business presentation to exchange notes, talk quietly in small groups, and come and go freely from the room as the presentation goes on. From a Western presenter's point of view, this behavior may be misunderstood as a lack of interest on the part of audience members. But from a Japanese perspective, it is not necessary for all members of a decision making team to be present for all portions of the presentation. The team trusts its members to gather the information needed from the presentation, even if no one team member heard the entire presentation from start to finish.

Another listening problem for a Westerner is often presented by Chinese hosts, for whom it is perfectly acceptable at meals or meetings including the Westerner to break into prolonged conversations in Mandarin or Cantonese. Even if a translator is present, these conversations typically go untranslated. The Westerner is left wondering whether to stare dumbly at his or her hosts, deep in Chinese conversation, to look to the translator for help, or to look elsewhere until the hosts again direct conversation to the Westerner in English or through the translator. Probably this last option is the best. The Westerner's visible signs of comfort during moments of untranslated conversation will come as a relief for Chinese business hosts. At the same time, the experience should alert the Westerner to feelings of being left out—feelings often encountered by Asian visitors to U.S. meetings and meals, where English buzzes on with little if any translation effort.

Cultures also have different conventions of *how long* audience members are typically willing to listen before offering reaction or input; *where* and *when* it is appropriate to listen to a sustained business presentation; and *what* they expect to hear in such presentations.

EXAMINING THE WAY YOU SPEAK

At the same time you are investigating useful foreign phrases, remember to examine *your* ways of speaking in an intercultural context. You can aid your hosts in understanding your business communications in three key ways.

1. Avoid slang and idioms.

2. Slow down your speech.

3. Check your listener's understanding of what you're saying.

Avoid Slang and Idioms

Learn to eliminate slang and idioms (including local or regional colloquial expressions) from the words you use for international business. Robert Bell, an international magnetic resonance specialist, makes the following comment.

> *When I travel to business meetings abroad, I have to remember that my ordinary mode of friendly conversation contains many idioms (such as "right on the money") that foreign colleagues will find strange and uninterpretable. I remind myself to speak plain vanilla English around those who don't know American English well.*

An American manager wrote the following sentence to a foreign businessperson with limited English skills: "By the way, I've shipped the computer order we discussed last week." The American manager was shocked to receive a fax from his foreign client: "What is the 'the way' you refer to? Urgent to know."

American English is rich in such easy-to-use idioms and expressions. Barron's *Guide to Cliches* (1999) lists more than 1,000 of them. For the sake of clear business dealings abroad, try to become aware of words and phrases that probably will be misunderstood abroad.

Slow Down Your Speech

Adjust the pace of your speaking to match the rate of comprehension of your foreign host. You will often do business with men and women abroad who have, through hard work, acquired quite a bit of English. If you rush ahead at the same speaking pace you would use with a native speaker, you unintentionally dash these people's efforts to communicate with you. Before leaving for an international trip, practice slowing down your speech without sounding patronizing. Look directly at the person to whom you are speaking so that he or she can see the words as they form on your lips and notice your facial and hand gestures.

Check for Comprehension

Some Americans, in speaking to foreign persons, frown quizzically as a visual way of asking, "Are you following me?" Try not to use the frown in this way. This puzzled look will often be misinterpreted as anger, criticism, or impatience.

Instead, when you want to check for comprehension, raise your eyebrows and give an inquiring smile. That visual gesture will produce either a nod of comprehension from your foreign friend or an indication that he or she has not understood. Learn to check often (in a polite way) to see whether your listener is comprehending. In a telephone conversation, for example, pause to ask "Am I being clear?" or "Do you understand?" or simply "Okay?"

In face-to-face conversations, including teleconferences, do not mistake a courteous smile on your listener's face or a nod as a sign of complete comprehension, and certainly not of complete agreement. Particularly in Asian and Latin American cultures, your listener will give you a smile simply as a polite gesture. Asian listeners may even nod and "yes" ("hai") repeatedly, all in an effort to show respect to you. All the while, they may almost entirely misunderstand what you are saying. Good barometers of such misunderstanding are the eyes. Watch to see whether your listener's eyes respond to your words. If you notice a glazed, lost look, back up and begin again in a simpler fashion. Another helpful technique is to politely ask the other party to say what he or she understood you to say. In working with a translator, this process is called back translation.

WHERE TO LEARN MORE ABOUT OTHER BUSINESS CULTURES

No businessperson can afford to learn about other cultures the hard way, through repeated blunders and mistakes. Fortunately, there are many ways to learn about other cultures before you step into your first intercultural business meeting or send off an important report to an international office. These techniques include obtaining information from the country's embassy or consulate, participating in cross-cultural training, asking people who have lived in or visited the country, and studying the language.

Information from Embassies and Consulates

Virtually all trading nations maintain experienced ambassadors and consuls in Washington, DC, and elsewhere in the United States. The commerce secretary at such embassies will furnish a great deal of information about the culture, customs, and business practices of the country. The secretary may also provide in-country contacts that can be enormously helpful in ensuring that your business visit is mutually profitable. See Chapters 7 and 8 for websites that will connect you directly with these valuable sources of cultural and business information.

Cross-Cultural Training

Many colleges, business associations, organizations, and independent consultants provide cross-cultural training. The websites listed in Chapter 10 will guide you to more specific information on the content, training method, locations, and costs of such training.

People Who Have Been There

Except for your own experience, the most valuable information you can get about another culture may come from someone whose background is similar to yours. Find out whether anyone in your company or college has visited the country in question. Find time to listen to stories of his or her experience. The ultimate authorities on a different culture are, of course, the people of that culture. Seek out their advice for how best to handle written and oral communications in the culture.

You can also seek information from the country's national airline serving your region (SwissAir, British Airways, Japan Airlines, and others). In addition, American banks that do business abroad and foreign banks in this country can prove helpful to you. Also consider the resources of the United States Chamber of Commerce. It publishes a number of booklets on trade relations.

Study the Language

Above all, begin language training for the culture you intend to visit. If you don't at least try to learn some aspects of the language, you will be totally dependent on a translator or isolated from conversation entirely. Don't be concerned that you haven't mastered the language entirely. Your foreign hosts will take it as a compliment that you are at least trying to learn their language. They probably will help you at every turn.

Chapter 4

Intercultural Opportunities Within the United States

◆

The cultural tools and sensitivities one develops for use outside U.S. borders are no less useful in business dealings with cultural groups and enclaves within the United States (the Cuban-American population of Miami, the Puerto Rican-American population of

New York, the Mexican-American population of Los Angeles, the Chinese-American population of San Francisco, and others.) We will look at each of these major groups in turn to remind ourselves of their large numbers and consequent economic power in the United States. Non-European ethnic groups will be of particular consequence in this regard, because their percentage in the U.S. population is projected to rise from its present 25 percent to 32 percent by 2010.

Our purpose in reviewing the demographics and dominant cultural features of these subcultures within the United States is the same as in our exploration of foreign cultures: to awaken insight, refine sensivity, and motivate strategy.

We do not claim, of course, that the subcultures described here are the only significant subcultures within the United States. These are, however, the subcultures identified most consistently by marketing experts as "culture sensitive" for business purposes—that is, highly reactive (pro or con) to marketing techniques and approaches that appeal or fail to appeal to the attitudes, beliefs, and feelings of the subculture.

HISPANICS

The Hispanic group (including those of Mexican, Puerto Rican, Cuban, and Central/South American ancestry) currently forms 11 percent of the U.S. population. Their numbers, the fastest growing of any ethnic group, are expected to rise to 14 percent by 2010. Their predominant communities are located in California, Arizona, Texas, Florida, and New York. Average family income levels vary widely among Hispanic subgroups:

	Average income
Mexican	$23,240
Puerto Rican	$18,008
Cuban	$31,439
Central/South American	$23,266
Other Hispanic	$27,382

An estimated 70 percent of Hispanics living in this country were born outside the United States. Cultural heritage is thus both fresh and strong within these communities. According to Bureau of the Census statistics, approximately 60 percent of Hispanic families used Spanish for communication in the home in the mid-1980s. By the mid-1990s, that number had grown to 70 percent. Spanish-language media (TV, radio, magazines, newspapers) have flourished on both a national and selected regional (Southwest, West, Southeast) basis.

Hispanic culture within the United States continues to be heavily influenced by the Roman Catholic religion. The culture values family, with an emphasis on the extended family more than is found in mainstream American culture. The macho tradition of the husband-dominant household is pervasive in the Hispanic culture, and must be taken into consideration when marketing to this culture. Hispanics tend to be avid partisans for soccer, boxing, and baseball. They tend to view U.S. citizenship as a blessing and have mixed emotions about the land of their birth or ancestry, where "things are worse."

ASIAN-AMERICANS

The Asian-American subculture now comprises 4 percent of the U.S. population and, by the year 2010, will grow to 6 percent. The group is made up of Chinese (24 percent), Filipino (20 percent), Japanese (12 percent), Korean (12 percent), Asian Indian (12 percent), Vietnamese (12 percent), and others (11 percent). On average, approximately two-thirds of this community use a language other than English for primary communication. More than half of all Asian-Americans live in California, New York, and Hawaii. The average income for Asian-Americans ($36,784) surpasses that of white Americans ($31,435).

Because of their diverse backgrounds, it is difficult at best to generalize about cultural aspects of Asian-Americans. Four attributes, however, seem to characterize most of the subgroups within this population.

◆ Husbands and wives are equally involved in bringing income into the home. Children often participate in family-owned businesses or in roles that are subordinate to relatives.

◆ Asian-Americans place an extremely high value on their children's education. A recent report from the Office of Admissions at the University of California–Berkeley pointed out that the entire freshman class at that institution could be filled by eligible 4.0 GPA Asian-American students were it not for the presence of Affirmative Action admissions policies for under-represented groups.

◆ Asian-Americans save at a higher rate than other Americans and place high value on financial security.

◆ Asian-Americans are conservative consumers, placing value on durability and quality.

AFRICAN-AMERICANS

The African-American group makes up 12 percent of the American population. Although the group's average household income is significantly below average for white Americans ($19,758 vs. $31,435), African-Americans have a large and growing middle class.

Family income	Percent
Greater than $99,000	1.4
$75,000–$99,999	3.1
$50,000–$74,999	10.3
$25,000–$49,999	29.3
$15,000–$24,999	18.4
Less than $15,000	37.5

Because African-Americans were among the earliest U.S. population, their values and lifestyles cannot be attributed in any direct way to underlying cultures in Africa, the Caribbean, or elsewhere. They spend heavily on personal care items, sports-related clothing and equipment, recorded music, automobiles, and clothing. On a percentage-of-income basis, they spend less heavily on home expenses.

Shopping ranks higher as a form of recreation with African-Americans (4th) than with whites (13th), and 60 percent of African-Americans identify respect as one of their most important reasons for selecting a retail store or service provider.

Although African-Americans generally have not retained strong political, economic, and social ties to African or Caribbean countries, they nevertheless have a strong sense of their ancestral roots and a general desire to learn more about those roots.

The African-American population has been especially welcoming to marketing efforts directed specifically to them. For example, Hallmark has launched a separate greeting card line for African-Americans; Mattel has a black version of its perpetually popular Barbie; and Esteé Lauder offers an extensive line of cosmetics for the African-American market.

Chapter 5

Specifics to Consider When Visiting Other Cultures

This chapter takes you on a walking tour of six common venues for intercultural contact. Here are the places and occasions where intercultural relations are spawned or spoiled for business. Because these venues are found in all cultures, the purpose in this chapter is *not* to guide your specific actions within particular cultures; that is the business of Chapter 6. Instead, we will endeavor here to *awaken sensitivities and powers of observation.* We hope that when you find yourself in the situations described in this chapter, an internal CAUTION signal will alert you to the presence of intercultural differences—and opportunities.

SITUATION 1: YOU GREET YOUR FOREIGN HOSTS OR ACQUAINTANCES

The U.S. ritual of initial greeting usually involves touching of some kind, ranging from a handshake at a first meeting to hugs and back-patting at more casual moments, especially among good friends. Learn in advance the appropriate greeting rituals for the culture you are visiting. In most cases, your physical actions (bowing, hand position, eye contact, and the like) will be more significant and certainly more memorable than the words you say. When meeting a group, pay particular attention to the *order* of expected greeting in the culture. Should you greet first the person highest in power in the organization? The eldest in the group? A woman before a man or vice versa?

In addressing your party by name, it is generally best to play it safe by using a new acquaintance's surname (Mr. Chan, Mr. Schwartz, Ms. Leger) until invited to do otherwise. It is also safe across virtually all cultures as part of the greeting ritual to pay a compliment to the person you are meeting—but a compliment on their courtesy, kindness, or hospitality in receiving you, or on the beauty of their city or country, not on their native dress, grooming, or other personal matters. (Notice that in the United States we often pay personal compliments. For example, a U.S. woman might say to another woman, "I love the pin you're wearing!")

SITUATION 2: YOU VISIT THE HOME OF AN ACQUAINTANCE

In the United States, we invite business acquaintances to our homes more freely than in most other cultures. In most cases, these visits are accompanied by food of some kind—drinks or dessert in the evening, lunch or dinner (rarely breakfast), and in some parts of the country an outdoor barbecue, clam bake, or fish fry.

Other cultures are much more likely to host you at an often-elaborate restaurant meal. If you are invited to visit a business associate at his or her home, consider it a special honor and sign of regard. To prepare for your visit, envision your evening (let's say) as it evolves step by step. First, imagine that you are greeted at the door by your hosts. Determine in advance if a gift is appropriate (usually yes) and, if so, what you should bring. Although flowers or wine are common gifts on such occasions in the United States, the *type* of flowers can matter greatly from culture to culture, and of course alcoholic gifts may be wholly inappropriate in some cultures.

Next, picture yourself entering the home. Is it appropriate to take off your shoes? If you comment on the beauty of the home or its contents, will it please or embarrass your hosts? A period of friendly small talk may precede the meal and continue throughout it. Find out in advance what sorts of topics are appropriate and which will be considered by your host to be intrusive, too business oriented, or too personal.

Now you are ready to sit down at the meal. Does your host guide you to a particular seat? If not, determine in advance which seat (facing the door? back to a window? at the end of the table or in the middle?) you should select as a guest. Also learn what conventions are expected with regard to the food served. Are compliments on each dish appropriate? Must you at least sample each dish? Should you converse while eating, or wait for a pause between courses for chat? What implements and utensils should you be prepared to use?

Finally, imagine yourself at the end of the occasion. You're thanking your hosts and bidding them goodnight or perhaps farewell. What specific compliments and words of thanks are appropriate at this juncture? For example, is it right or wrong to compliment your hosts on their beautiful children? Their lovely home? Their art collection or other displayed possessions? The meal itself? The answers to these questions vary around the world. The point here is to find out in advance what will be appropriate rather than to presume that U.S. customs prevail.

SITUATION 3: YOU ATTEND A MEETING AND GIVE A PRESENTATION

In the United States, a visitor is usually given a prominent place on the meeting agenda and is warmly introduced to the group before he or she speaks. The meeting begins on time; to be late without a good reason is considered a sign of disrespect and unprofessionalism. Attendees are expected to sit throughout the presentation, unless an individual emergency requires that one or more leave the room. Questions are usually reserved for the end of the presentation, unless invited earlier by the speaker.

What about meetings and presentations in other cultures? Does a meeting set for 10 A.M. begin on time? Will meeting participants come and go from the room during your presentation—and if so, do they mean any disrespect or lack of interest by this behavior? What does it mean if they talk among themselves even as you are speaking? Is it important that they may not look at you during your entire speech? Does your posture as you sit or stand send powerful messages in the culture? (The American habits of shifting often in the chair, folding arms, visibly suppressing a yawn, and perhaps slouching are interpreted in many cultures as insulting and unprofessional.) For your sanity and success, learn the answers to these questions in the culture you are visiting *before* you make a business presentation.

As for your speech itself, what topics are traditional openers in the culture? What topics should not be introduced until later, or not at all? Should you attempt interaction (discussion, for example) with your business audience during your speech? If you are using an interpreter, how can you tell that the translation process is going smoothly for your listeners? Should you gesture freely and employ

some humor, or should your presentation manner be strictly formal? Finally, evaluate your expectations for your presentation. In the culture at hand, can you expect frank feedback on your speech at its conclusion? Will action be immediately forthcoming based on your ideas or delayed, perhaps for a long period, for consideration and consultation? More than one American businessperson has walked away from a foreign meeting feeling that his or her presentation was an abysmal failure—only to learn later that cultural behaviors and cues had been misinterpreted.

SITUATION 4: YOU LOOK IN THE MIRROR

Dress for business and business-related occasions varies widely in the United States from power suits for men and women (conservative, usually expensive businesswear) to the corporate-casual look with slacks and sweaters to the jeans-and-T-shirt uniform popular in many hi-tech companies.

In many cultures, how you dress is an indelible mark of your place and power within your organization, your professionalism, and your respect for your hosts. Your favorite hat or an eye-catching tie may be exceedingly distracting and mystifying to your cultural hosts if worn to a business occasion. Short-sleeve shirts or blouses may seem absolutely sensible to you in a warm-weather, humid climate, but they may send the wrong signals entirely to your foreign hosts, who may have dutifully donned their suits.

The full range of appearance options, from beards and moustaches to styles of makeup, accessorizing, and piercing, should be evaluated for their effect on the culture you intend to visit. Will an expensive ring, necklace, or earrings be seen as ostentatious? Will open-toed shoes or sandals be seen as stylish or inappropriate? Aids associated with disabilities (wheelchairs, leg braces, canes, for example) may elicit frequent comments, questions, and expressions of concern in some cultures, as will the dental braces now becoming common for U.S. adults.

SITUATION 5: YOU DON'T SPEAK THE LANGUAGE

If fluency in a foreign language was an absolute prerequisite for international business travel, few U.S. businesspeople would be doing deals abroad. Compared to most other nations, U.S. citizens are remarkably monolingual. It takes a bit of effort, therefore, to prepare even a modest set of visitor phrases in the language(s) of the country you're visiting.

With the possible exception of France, where citizens sometimes prefer no French rather than bad French, your attempt to communicate in the language of the land will be appreciated by your foreign hosts. Here is a suggested list of 20 useful phrases to master. In seeking translations for the culture of your choice, be sure to go beyond pronouncing dictionaries to actual recordings of these phrases by native speakers. The way a word looks in the dictionary, even with phonetic markings, is often very different from the way it should sound. This is especially true for tonal languages such as Mandarin, in which the same sound can have dramatically different meanings depending on the pitch you use. (Recordings of the following phrases, on audiotape and CD, can be found in the foreign languages section at most bookstores.)

Hello.

It is an (honor/pleasure) to meet you.

How are you?

I am very well.

Thank you (extended, Thank you for your kindness/courtesy/ hospitality).

I like this food very much.

My hotel is very comfortable.

It is an honor/pleasure to do business with you.

This is very impressive/beautiful (said of a building, natural scenery, and so on.)

I agree.

I respectfully disagree.

Yes.

No.

Let's talk further.

You have a lovely family.

Please direct me to the restroom.

I must leave at (time).

I will contact you soon.

Good-bye.

I enjoyed visiting (country or region name).

Mastering these phrases may take a few hours spread out over several days prior to your departure. Your efforts, however, will be repaid many times over by the quick rapport you will build with your foreign hosts. In addition, you will find that your hosts will be eager to teach you additional phrases, once you have demonstrated your competence in a few phrases and your interest in learning more.

SITUATION 6: CONVERSATION TURNS TO HISTORY

Typically, Americans do not know what it means to experience "living history." For example, over dinner or drinks we do not usually debate the merits of Washington's decision to cross the Delaware River or the circumstances of Cabrillo's first visit to what was to become California. We may know these items of history, but they do not matter to us as day-to-day influences on our feelings and actions.

Not so in many other countries. Feuds, wars, rivalries, deceptions, and heroism that took place hundreds of years ago are actively on the minds and tongues of your foreign hosts, as a visit to any Irish pub will attest. And because versions of history are held passionately by your hosts, you should become knowledgeable about a country's or region's history prior to your visit. Once there, show interest in matters of history raised by your host and, in general, avoid questions or statements that imply partisanship. Your host in Beijing, for example, may be uncomfortable with questions reflecting your U.S. view of the events at Tiananmen Square or associated human rights issues.

This is not to say that you must leave your mind and conscience at home when you travel abroad. Realize, however, that your political questions and comments will not be taken as chat by your foreign hosts, to whom history matters as much as money matters to Americans.

In each of the preceding six situations, the advice has been given to learn as much as you can before departing on business travel. But how and where can such learning take place? The best source is extended conversation with a native of the land you plan to visit. This person can often be located in your company, through the foreign languages departments at local colleges (with an honorarium for services), or with the help of the country's embassy or consulate (see contact information at the end of this book). If you can't find a native informant, seek out someone who has visited the country or read books, magazine articles, or Internet entries. Armed with such knowledge, you can avoid the painful and, for business purposes, what might be the very damaging experience of learning by cultural mistakes.

Chapter 6

Intercultural Business Tips by Area Experts

For detailed suggestions on how to adapt to the cultural expectations of major trading nations, we turn to those who know best: businesspeople who have spent their business lives in these cultures. In the space available, we have endeavored to collect valuable tips from around the world, with special emphasis on Asian business cultures with which Western readers may be less familiar than European cultures.

BELGIUM

1. Business negotiations are often conducted over meals, but only very elaborate fine dining.

2. Business culture in Belgium tends to be Germanic in the Dutch-speaking northern region of Flanders. It tends to be more Latin in the French-speaking areas of Bruxelles and Wallonia.

3. Belgians tend to be cosmopolitan and born merchants since the thirteenth century. Import/export accounts for 90 percent of the country's GDP.

4. Belgian employees are conservative, hardworking, dutiful, and ethical. They keep to the middle of the road and rarely show aggressive, passionate, or extravagant traits.

5. Belgians' small family-business tradition and laws for inheriting wealth have resulted in a very high household net worth—$300,000 per household—double that of the Netherlands and four times that of the United States.

6. Belgians also have one of the world's highest savings rates. Over 60 percent of Belgians own their own homes.

7. Frequent changes in tax laws and regulations of all kinds are accepted as normal by Belgians, due to their multicultural political system and complex legislative structure.

8. An employee's take-home pay is small compared to his total cost to the company due to heavy social security burdens. Employers find hiring and firing equally unattractive and difficult. The government tries to control black-market employment, but it is still common and may be as high as 17 percent of the GDP.

Jan Melsen
Butterfield & Butterfield
Bruxelles, Belgium

CHINA

1. Exchange of gifts is part of the culture. It is important that you have a gift for your counterpart as well as his or her superior when you first meet. The gift need not be of great value but it must be enough to show your sincerity and good wishes.

2. Patience is needed because very often it takes time before a deal can be completed pending a decision from the highest level.

3. A willingness to make necessary compromises is an effective way of reaching a quick business deal.

4. You can build a good relationship by being generous in your praise for the past achievements of the organization you are dealing with. For this purpose, background information is needed before your meeting.

5. A word or two in Chinese at your first meeting *(ni hau, xie xie)* can help break the ice.

6. Friendship and mutual connections (relations) are two short-cuts to successful business cooperation.

7. A decision is often not likely to be made at a conference table, even though those present may be high-ranking officials. It is often the case that they will discuss the matter after the meeting and get back to you at a later date.

8. The first meeting is likely to be of a social nature, which serves to pave the way for the establishment of a relationship. Do not expect to go into anything substantial at the first meeting.

9. With some enterprises, the highest level person in charge may have to take care of day-to-day routines as well as all-around development plans. He or she will leave the matter of attending

meetings to his or her representative(s). His or her appearance at such meetings is merely a gesture of goodwill and of high hopes that he or she has for the outcome of the meetings.

10. Enterprises are of two types in China: state-owned and privatized. Generally speaking, the former are more conservative and the latter aggressive. With the economic reforms now sweeping the country, management and operation of businesses have undergone great changes. The legend that state-owned enterprises will never go broke does not exist anymore.

11. The organizational position indicated on your counterpart's name card may be puzzling and may not offer a clue as to the structure of the organization in question. In this case your guide or interpreter might prove to be a great help in better understanding organization. A person with a puzzling title may prove to be a key figure in the success of a trade negotiation.

Ming Xuan Liu
China Resources, Ltd.

CHINA

(MORE TIPS . . .)

1. When negotiating a joint venture or any type of long-term contractual relationship with the Chinese party, ensure that at least one or two key members of the negotiation team will remain in place after execution of the contract, preferably actually living in China, but if not, making numerous visits each year.

2. Ensure that the foreign representative who is living in China or visits regularly has direct visible support from the very top levels of the foreign company. The best way to convey this message is for the number one or number two person in the company to visit China regularly.

3. *Guan Xi* (a personal relationship that is helpful in business) cannot be established only when one needs help from a bureaucrat or ministry. It should be established over a long period of time and is most safely relied upon after the establishment of a friendly relationship in a noncrisis mode.

4. When possible, establish a wholly foreign-owned entity rather than a joint venture. The benefits of the joint venture are greatly overrated and the downside cannot be emphasized enough.

5. In documenting a transaction, follow international or Western standards, because the local partner in China can become incredibly legalistic in the event of controversy or dispute. Normally the Western or international standards in documentation provide for much more detail including resolution of conflicts and procedures for exiting the transaction under certain circumstances.

6. The translation of written materials and translators involved in negotiations are very important. Do not underestimate the importance of obtaining first-rate translation support. Be sure that such support is paid for by you rather than the other side.

7. Obtain independent outside consulting advice with regard to approval procedures. Know the do's and don'ts of the regulatory scheme. Do not rely totally on your local partner, who often-times is not completely familiar with the legal and regulatory issues.

8. As a general rule, it is better to engage in a variety of smaller transactions in China over a period of time rather than to put all your eggs in one large transaction basket. This will accomplish a broader learning curve at a lower price.

David A. Livdahl
Graham & James Ltd.

CZECH REPUBLIC

1. This is a white male-dominated business community and society in general. Prepare for this reality in staffing your business mission.

2. Do not underestimate the importance and value of political connections here.

3. Corruption is viewed as widespread and prevalent. Caution: some government and business leaders are of old vintage, and are more interested in their personal objectives than in improving their organizations.

4. This country placed last in insider trading and stock market quality in the Global Competitive Report of 1998.

5. Unlike ten years ago, most businesspeople here are able to communicate in English now.

6. It may be difficult scheduling meetings for Friday afternoon because most Czechs prefer leaving for their weekend houses early on Friday.

7. People here smoke in meetings without asking permission.

8. Lunch is not a grab-and-go sandwich. It is a full-sized meal and it often takes an hour or more. Alcohol may be abundantly served.

9. When it comes to small talk, be knowledgeable about Czech players in the National Hockey League. They are national heroes.

10. Academic titles are still considered very important. You may see several titles listed on a business card.

11. Unless you're invited to use the first name, always refer to your business partner by the academic title and the last name. If they do not have an academic title, use Mr. or Ms.

Peter Palecek
Arthur D. Little International

GERMANY

1. If you decide to use a bit of German, be sure to maintain the *Sie* (formal) designation for "you" rather than the informal *du* in business relations, even after a long period of business dealings. German businesspeople will feel embarrassed if you address them inappropriately with *du*. Let them decide when the relationship should use the *du* designation.

2. Use a businessperson's last name until the person requests that you call them by their first name. This latter option may not happen for years in many business relationships.

3. Germans draw a strict line between work life and family life. They rarely talk about their families at work and should not be asked to do so by a visitor.

4. In business conversations, Germans like to come to the point. This is not intended to be rude or confrontational. Instead, it reflects the German desire to base relationships on facts and certainties.

5. Germans may seem to focus on the negative to a much greater degree than American businesspeople. It is almost a national pastime to complain about politics, a recent soccer game, food, or other matters. Do not be misled by this habit. In fact, Germans enjoy life deeply.

6. Recycling is a matter of political correctness in Germany, and should not be ridiculed or rejected by a visitor. Germans have developed a complicated system for recycling everything from plastic to glass and paper.

7. In terms of service, German retail shops (except high-priced shops) tend to lag behind the expectations of American retailers. A German clerk who does not give much advice or show much interest in your patronage is not being rude, but is simply doing the job, as defined by his or her business culture.

8. When invited to an occasion, it is a good idea to bring flowers or a bottle of wine. Germans use the expression "contributions are welcome" to indicate that you are expected to bring something to drink or eat. Feel free to check with your host about what would be best to bring.

Anka Turner

HONG KONG

1. In Chinese cultures it is inappropriate to give gifts that have sharp edges. A letter opener, for example, would be inappropriate. This is generally true for all sharp or pointed objects.

2. Meals are important to the Chinese. It is important that if you are the host you are there to greet your guests. A guest should not arrive early and thereby embarrass a host who may not be available to greet his arrival.

3. At a Chinese table, where one sits is very important. The host would ordinarily sit in the most appropriate chair with his back to the most comfortable corner. A host woud never sit with his back to the door. By order of importance or respect, guests are seated alternately to the right and then the left of the host until the individuals sitting directly across the round table are opposite the host. The host will talk to those near him or her and not across the table unless addressing the entire table. Do not expect any important discussions to take place with anyone not seated directly next to the host, as others would hear.

Once while having lunch with Robert Kuok Hock Nein, Chairman of the Kuok Group, he seated my young children to his right and left as a sign of his respect for my family. The youngest, age 7, was seated to his right. This show of respect is an extremely important issue.

4. What one orders from the menu is important in showing not how much you can spend but how much you value your guests.

5. When attending business dinners, both men and women should dress modestly, without their best baubles. Save those for charity balls.

6. Let your host be the first to pour your tea; you can reciprocate on the next round. The Hong Kong Chinese have a quaint way of tapping their fingers on the table as a gesture of saying "thank you" to the tablemate who pours.

7. Never underestimate the importance of a prominent Chinese person accepting an invitation for a meal. It may mean they wish to show respect for you personally, for your company, or they may want something from you. They do not attend dinners for a free meal. Being seen in public with you is an important consideration and statement, at least at the highest levels of business. At lower level business lunches, the atmosphere is more Western and casual.

Randolph Guthrie
Hong Kong
Beaufort Hotels

ISRAEL

1. In Israel people work on Sundays and usually not on Fridays. No shops or public transportation operate from early afternoon Friday until Saturday night.

2. When writing a résumé, the first line will be your name, and directly after will be your date of birth and family facts (marital status and number of kids).

3. In interviews people tend to ask personal questions as well as professional ones. Interviewees may be asked about their partner's occupation, whether they have kids, and, if not, when they plan to have kids.

4. All the procedures in Israel are less formal. Many times people do things by intuition and not by a whole process.

5. People are direct. If they think you failed in something they may tell you this to your face. If someone totally disagrees with you in a meeting he may say "you don't know what you're talking about" in front of other people, without wrapping it with compliments.

6. People in Israel don't have credit history. Almost everyone gets a credit card upon opening an account. It is very common for people to live with an overdraft in the bank.

7. People usually dress less formally. Full suits are rare, and ties are only for special occasions.

8. Army issues: All men in Israel serve for three years, and women for two years. Men have to go to reserve duties for up to one month every year until they are 45 years old (losing time at work).

9. In casual meetings, politics is a common issue to discuss. People are influenced in their daily lives by the political situation. The radio has a new update every hour. Most people watch the evening news on TV (8:00 every night).

Nurit Gery

INDIA

1. It is important to know that the majority of Indian businesspeople believe in long-term business relations.

2. They are religious in nature. Therefore, showing interest and respect for their values and culture is profitable for both partners.

3. When negotiating with an Indian company, it is good to get right to the point, and even better to be polite.

4. Indian companies prefer résumés to be formal and conservative in layout, font, and style. The usual order of résumé topics is name, address, age, sex, objective, education, work experience, and extracurricular activities.

5. If a businessman or woman invites you to have dinner or lunch with his or her family it means that the business deal is almost completed and that your host is interested in establishing a personal relationship with you. When invited for family outings it is always advisable to take a gift along.

6. One thing to be noticed is that in the traditional Indian business circle, most of the decisions are made by men, and women help facilitate them. Now the scenario is changing, but slowly.

7. The Indian business environment is conservative and traditional in nature.

8. In a hierarchy the ideas usually flow from the top to the lower level and in rare cases from lower to top level.

9. There is a jungle of bureaucracy in public sector establishments. If you are dealing with these institutions and offices, expect progress to be slow. Remain polite and be persistent.

Charanjeet Ajmani

JAPAN

1. It is appreciated that you have studied several Japanese greeting sentences and use them when you meet Japanese counterparts.

2. To succeed in the long term with business dealings in Japan, you or your staff must be able to negotiate in Japanese.

3. Bowing in Japan is as common as shaking hands, winking, or hugging in Western societies, or as common as the praying gesture in India and Thailand. Therefore, be prepared to bow with dignity in Japan whenever you greet and want to express intimacy, understanding, agreement, respect, gratitude, apology, or a requested favor. Bowing is used frequently during meetings. You may often find yourself bowing ten times or more at a single, ordinary business meeting. Bowing in Japan is not a sign of obedience, but instead a form of body language to express mutual understanding. Bowing is reciprocal. Even the emperor bows to his subordinate.

4. An invitation to lunch or dinner is important in Japan. Businesspeople do not accept invitations from counterparts they do not trust. If you want to invite a Japanese businessperson to lunch, choose a restaurant of your own culture (these can be found in the Yellow Pages or through your concierge). During the meal, speak freely about your cultural background. Then it is likely that your Japanese counterpart will invite you to a Japanese restaurant and explain to you some aspects of Japanese culture. International friendships always begin with introducing one's culture. People with only business on their minds cannot make friends in Japan or succeed in business relationships. During meals, use as many Japanese sentences as you remember. Bow often, when appropriate.

5. During a business meal or meeting, you should begin by giving your counterparts information that they find educational, helpful, important, or entertaining. To give such information, you will need to study what kind of information your counterparts appreciate.

6. When negotiations start, do not merely express the excellence and advantages of your products. Also show how your product can bring profit, credit, and fortune to your counterpart's business. You must know Japanese economy, business, and product lines well in order to show your counterparts how your product can help them.

7. Whom you know in Japan is very important for business. If you know a highly respected, important person in Japan, use his or her endorsement and connection. Before you start an important negotiation, make contact with an appropriate person, ask for a consultation, and then ask if you can use the endorsement and

connection to further your business efforts. This formula of using connections is regularly used by Japanese businesspeople.

8. Do not show your anger, bad mood, or short temper to your business counterpart. Almost all Japanese businesspeople have attended Emotional Intelligence (EI) seminars, either sent by their companies or through voluntary attendance.

9. A good website for further information about business dealings in Japan is *http://home.jcic.or.jp*

Makoto Asabuki
Japan Center for
International Communications

KOREA

1. Be relatively formal in meetings. Sit up straight and maintain decorum.

2. Always exchange business cards when you first meet. Offer and accept them with your right hand. They are an individual's "face," so treat them with respect.

3. Meetings open with a ritualistic offer of coffee or tea. It is rude to refuse, so always accept, but do not feel obliged to drink.

4. Limit conversation to small talk in the meeting until the tea time is over.

5. When you present your corporate materials to introduce yourself and your firm, you signal the start of serious discussion.

6. Build up to your main point. Cutting to the chase reduces the impact of your message.

7. Summarize your key points at the end of the meeting so that all parties understand the next steps and timing.

8. Highly organize your presentation. Deliver your points in short, clear, outline form. Keep your grammar simple. Enunciate clearly and speak slowly. Avoid metaphors and idioms.

9. Use the family name and title in addressing people (for example, Director Kim).

10. Use open-ended questions to ensure that you get accurate information. Otherwise it is too easy for the respondent to say yes or no, and thereby hide misunderstanding.

Peter Underwood
IRC Limited

KOREA

(MORE TIPS . . .)

1. Having dinner is a sign of recognition as a business partner.

2. Business decisions are often made during meals, but much more often at dinner than at lunch.

3. If you are the seller in negotiations, you should pay for the meal.

4. Listening is a sign of respect and discipline. Do not talk more than your client.

5. Seating at virtually all meetings and other occasions will be carefully planned. The most important person will sit in the best or center position.

6. You should talk about your company with pride but downplay your own achievements and abilities. Bragging about yourself will make you seem naive.

7. Repeated and routine visits to the country will be taken as a positive sign and will pay off in negotiations. You do not need a business purpose to visit.

8. Never try to handle all business matters over the telephone. Face-to-face meetings are important as a sign that you take business negotiations seriously.

9. Do not ask the age of your business counterparts in Korea. Age is a very important factor for evaluating someone in Korean culture. Asking someone's age can be as offensive as asking how much money they have in the bank.

10. Do not let your secretary call your client for you. Dial the number yourself.

11. Do not sit back in your chair with legs crossed. It can be taken as showing a bad attitude.

12. If you must say no, do so cautiously. A blunt "No" can be an end to business negotiations.

Tae Young Chung
Hyunda, Precision America, Inc.

SAUDI ARABIA

1. Although reputed to be among the world's wealthiest populations, many Saudi businesspeople view themselves as struggling to achieve their business goals, due in large part to the low price of crude oil in recent years. Therefore, do not approach negotiations in the false belief that Saudis consider themselves to be wealthy beyond concern.

2. Saudi businesspeople usually make an effort to get to know prospective business partners on an informal basis before entering into formal business meetings and negotiations. Do not be surprised if you are invited to an informal but important meeting over dinner before any scheduled business meeting.

3. Appointments are approximate, not precise. Do not be offended if your Saudi host is late for a meeting or unprepared to receive you exactly at the appointed time.

4. Networking is vastly important in Saudi Arabia. You will be trusted and respected to the extent that you know and have dealings with many key players in the Saudi business world.

5. Gifts are not considered bribery, but simply a means of showing appreciation and extending friendship.

6. Gender is segregated in business. Males work with males, females with females. Only in a few companies and fields, such as medical institutions, do men work side by side with women.

7. Everything is negotiable, from the smallest pricetag in a local market to the largest fee or contract amount in a business meeting. Saudis expect you to negotiate and will do so themselves—vigorously.

8. Almost all parts of the country are completely safe for walking or travel by cab. Feel free to explore. Your Saudi hosts will appreciate your interest in their culture and environment.

9. In doing business with a major company, it is appropriate to ask for a car and driver to enable you to find your way to business appointments at various places. Making your own way can be frustrating and confusing.

10. Contrary to popular belief, weather is not uniformly hot throughout Saudi Arabia. Get to know the locations you plan to visit, and pack clothes accordingly. Some locations are cold!

11. Carry your passport or a copy of your passport at all times. You will be asked for it often.

Ahmed Ismail

SINGAPORE

1. It is considered disrespectful to address your more senior business associates or counterparts by their first names, unless requested to do so.

2. It is unwise to adopt a confrontational approach during dealing, as Singaporeans generally like to avoid altercations.

3. Establishing and maintaining personal relationships is an essential prerequisite to completing business deals.

4. As a mark of respect and sincerity, business cards must be personally handed to each person in the room. Extend both your hands from chest level to everyone, except your own colleagues, at the meeting. The cards must also be received in this manner. Read the card with interest and acknowledge the person giving the card.

5. The hosts of a meal (whether male or female) should stand up upon the arrival of guests (whether male or female) and approach and greet them.

6. It is inappropriate to smoke or offer a cigarette to a business associate without first inquiring if the associate minds.

7. It is inappropriate to give gifts of significant value to business associates without first ascertaining the policy of the firm or company in which the associate works.

8. Telephone calls to business associates should be made personally and not through a secretary. The caller should be on the line when the business associate picks up the line.

9. It is not polite to decline invitations from a business associate to social events.

10. Punctuality at all meetings and timeliness in completing requests for work is a mark of professionalism in Singapore.

11. Do not assume that your spouse or partner is included when you are invited to a business reception or dinner.

12. Throughout Asia, a business dinner may include a karaoke session. It is impolite not to participate with gusto.

13. When you are invited to a dinner, do not go empty-handed. Bring an appropriate gift for your host.

Lucien Wong
Allen & Gledhill

Peter Foo
Peninsula Holdings, Inc.

TAIWAN

1. Asking personal questions in Taiwan is considered friendly, not nosy. Expect to be asked whether you are married, how many children you have, and even how much money you make.

2. When bringing a gift, give something like imported liquor, perfume, or chocolate. These are highly appropriate gifts for business partners.

3. Avoid direct criticism of people, even your own subordinates, when in the company of Chinese. Your Chinese hosts stress polite manners and smooth relations.

4. When you receive a gift, it is impolite to open it in front of the giver. It will seem greedy. Thank the person, put the gift aside, open it later, then express appropriate thanks again.

5. Do not lose your temper. Smiling is an appropriate response in an embarrassing situation.

6. When handing a piece of paper to someone, use both hands. Handing it with one hand only is considered rude.

7. Flattering your hosts is considered proper and advantageous. You can praise them for intelligence, humor, beauty, and the like.

8. Learn to use chopsticks. Proper etiquette demands that you hold your rice bowl close to your face rather than leaving it on the table in typical Western fashion.

9. Remove your shoes when visiting your hosts' home. When using the bathroom, use the set of slippers usually provided.

Dr. Elton See Tan
America California Bank

TAIWAN

(MORE TIPS . . .)

1. A good relationship (guan xi) can be developed once trust has been established between parties.

2. Don't put your business counterparts on the spot in the presence of others. Embarrassment will cause them to lose face among their peers.

3. Try to learn a few words of greeting and courtesy in Mandarin Chinese. These will help you break the ice when you first meet your business partner.

4. Have your business card printed in Chinese on the reverse side, but be sure you can rely on accuracy from your translator!

5. When you meet someone for the first time, be prepared for the formal exchange of business cards. Always use both hands to receive or give cards. Show interest in the card you receive.

6. Time is money in Taiwan. Businesspeople like quick decision making and action. Quotations, corporate information, and product brochures will be expected during a meeting.

7. When you are a guest at a meal, enjoy what may seem to be exotic foods. Your hosts will appreciate your willingness to try new things.

8. Your best defense is not superior business knowledge but respect. If you are caught in an awkward situation, simply confess your ignorance and ask for help.

Jason Hou
ELSI Taiwan Language Schools

THAILAND

1. Most businessmen and women in Thailand have a Chinese mixed ancestry. You may apply the cultural assumptions and tactics used for the Chinese to the Thais.

2. Relationships and friendships are very important in business dealings. People are looking for long-term business relationships. It is considered good to take time to build up such relationships.

3. Being connected is also another crucial part of business in Thailand. Who you know is as important as what you know.

4. Written contracts can be meaningless here. Trust is more important than such contracts. However, you should check to see if the people you are dealing with are reputable. This is not difficult because the business community in Thailand is quite small. You can check their record from a few sources, including a bank, trade association, industry association, and so on.

5. Make room for compromise in all negotiations. Thais like to feel they got the best deal possible. Therefore, always be prepared for a last-minute request or negotiation.

6. Be sure that your business partners fully understand all points. Thais will tend to be quiet and not ask for clarification, even though they do not fully understand.

7. Be fair, helpful, and giving. This builds up relationships and will not be forgotten by your Thai associates. Don't base business negotiations on following strict rules. Be reasonable and flexible.

8. Avoid confrontation. Thais tend to be rather passive, soft-spoken, and accommodating in nature. They feel uncomfortable with confrontation.

9. Don't be upset if your foreign hosts suddenly revert to their own language and leave you sitting there wondering what is going on. They mean no disrespect to you.

10. You will often hear the phrase *mai pen rai*, which means *never mind*. Sins and misdemeanors are readily forgiven here.

11. You will not be questioned. What you say goes. Think carefully before giving instructions or information.

Thiraphong Chansiri
Thai Union
Frozen Products Co.

Gregory J. Meadows
General Manager
The Sukhothai Bangkok

TURKEY

1. Cash is still king in Turkey. Checks are not generally trusted, especially for smaller transactions.

2. Since Turkey as a republic is only 75 years old, most companies are relatively young. Those with a history of several decades are highly respected.

3. Trust is a person-to-person matter, not based on one's credit references alone. Never underestimate the value of sincere, thoughtful, interpersonal relations when doing business in Turkey.

4. Turkish people are usually eager to escape business formalities and procedures in favor of expedited dealings based on trust. As good relations develop, it is not uncommon for Turkish businesspeople to invite international partners to stay at their homes during business visits. This openness is the Turkish way of building lasting relationships.

5. Turkish people hold many aspects of Western, and especially American, business and cultural life in awe. They generally approach negotiations and business dealings with great respect for their Western partners.

6. Because business relationships overlap so quickly with social relationships and friendships in Turkey, it is important for the Western businessperson to avoid making unfounded and unenforceable assumptions about the business deal at hand. Terms should be stated often and understood by all.

Ayca Katun

UNITED KINGDOM

1. Avoid handing out business cards at the beginning of meetings or when first introduced to someone (unless a card is requested). The business card ritual is generally considered a parting gesture or side thought.

2. When meeting someone senior to you in status for the first time, you address the person as Mr. or Ms., followed by their surname. If the person were of similar or lower hierarchical status than yourself, you may address the person by their first name.

3. Any meeting conducted over lunch or after working hours would commonly take place in the local pub. Be prepared to buy a few rounds of drinks.

4. Dress code for U.K. companies is typically more formal than for U.S. companies. Coat and tie are almost always expected. Even for occasional informal Fridays in U.K. companies, formal dress codes apply whenever meetings are scheduled.

5. You will encounter (and may use) "Cheers" as a frequent and acceptable ending for an e-mail message or conversation.

6. General working hours for U.K. companies are between 9 A.M. and 5 P.M. Always make an appointment well in advance of any visit.

7. Take time to acquaint yourself with standard U.K. business terms: GMT, Greenwich Meridian Time, is attached to time designations; AOB, any other business, appears at the end of many meeting agendas; tea is another word for dinner; and football always means soccer.

Asad Qizilbash

Chapter 7

Getting Help from Foreign Embassies in the United States

The primary public relations and business relations arm of a country is probably its embassy or consulate. By using the web addresses provided in this chapter you can:

◆ obtain the latest on-line information about the country or region;

◆ receive a wealth of printed materials on the country's people, culture, economy, and business practices;

◆ get in touch with the country's commercial officers and attaches, who in turn can expedite your efforts to meet vendors and potential clients in your industry;

◆ learn about the country's current trade interests and initiatives, programs for partnering with foreign businesses, tariffs, and other practical business matters.

Starting the flow of such information is just a few keystrokes away on the Internet.

FOREIGN EMBASSIES IN THE UNITED STATES

Afghanistan   *www.afghan-government.com*

Angola   *www.angola.org/*

Australia   *www.austemb.org/*

Bangladesh   *www.undp.org/missions/bangladesh/*

Belarus   *www.undp.org/missions/belarus/*

Belgium   *www.belgium-emb.org/usa/*

Bolivia   *www.interbol.com/consul.htm*

Bosnia Herzegovina   *www.bosnianembassy.org/*

Brazil   *www.brasil.emb.nw.dc.us/*

Cambodia   *www.embassy.org/cambodia/*

Canada   *www.cdnemb-washdc.org/*

China   *www.china-embassy.org/*

Colombia   *www.colombiaemb.org/*

Costa Rica   *www.costarica.com/embassy/*

Croatia   *www.croatiaemb.org/*

Cyprus   *www.trncwashdc.org/*

Czech Republic   *www.czech.cz/washington/*

Denmark   *www.denmarkemb.org/*

Dominican Republic   *www.domrep.org/*

Ecuador   *www.ecuador.org/ecuador/*

El Salvador   *www.elsalvadorguide.com/consalvamia/*

Eritrea   *www.usia.gov/posts/eritrea/*

Estonia   *www.estemb.org/*

Ethiopia   *www.nicom.com/~ethiopia/*

European Union   *www.eurunion.org/*

Faroe Island   *www.denmarkemb.org/*

Finland   *www.finland.org/*

Georgia   *server.parliament.ge/foreign/geemb3.html*

Germany   *www.germany-info.org/*

Ghana   *www.usembassy.org.gh/*

Great Britain   *www.britain-info.org/*

Greece   *www.greekembassy.org/*

Greenland   *www.denmarkemb.org/*

Haiti   *www.mnsinc.com/embassy/*

Hong Kong   *www.hketony.org/*

Hungary   *www.hungaryemb.org/*

Iceland   *www.iceland.org/*

India   *www.indianembassy.org/*

Indonesia   *www.kbri.org/*

Iran   *www.daftar.org/*

Iraq   *www.undp.org/missions/iraq/*

Ireland   *www.irelandemb.org/*

Israel   *www.israelemb.org/*

Italy   *www.italyemb.org/*

Jamaica   *www.caribbean-online.com/jamaica/embassy/washdc/*

Japan   *www.embjapan.org/*

Jordan   *www.jordanembassyus.org/*

Kenya   *www.embassyofkenya.com/*

Kuwait   *www.kuwait.info/nw.dc.us/*

Krygyzstan   *www.kyrgyzstan.org/*

Laos   *www.laoembassy.com/*

Latvia   *www.seas.gwu.edu/guest/latvia/*

Lesotho   *www.undp.org/missions/lesotho/*

Liberia   *www.liberiaemb.org/*

Libya   *www.undp.org/missions/libya/*

Lithuania   *www.ltembassyus.org/*

Luxembourg   *www.undp.org/missions/luxembourg/*

Macedonia   *ourworld.compuserve.com/homepages/yuembassy/*

Madagascar   *www.embassy.org/madagascar/*

Malaysia   *www.undp.org/missions/malaysia/*

Maldives   *www.undp.org/missions/maldives/*

Mali   *maliembassy-usa.org/*

Marshall Islands   *www.rmiembassyus.org/*

Mauritania   *www.embassy.org/mauritania/*

Mauritius   *www.idsonline.com/usa/embasydc.html*

Mexico   *www.quicklink.com/mexico/*

Micronesia   *www.fsmembassy.org/*

Moldova   *www.moldova.org/*

Monaco   *www.monaco.mc/usa/*

Mongolia   *members.aol.com/monemb/*

Mozambique   *www.undp.org/missions/mozambique/*

Nepal   *www.newweb.net/nepal_embassy/*

Netherlands   *www.netherlands-embassy.org/*

New Zealand   *www.emb.com/nzemb/*

Norway   *www.norway.org/*

Pakistan   *www.pakistan-embassy.com/*

Papua New Guinea   *www.diamondhead.net/pgn.htm*

Peru   *www.heuristika.com/consulado-peru/*

Philippines   *www.philconsul-la.org/*

Poland   *homepage.interaccess.com/~comconpl/*

Romania   *www.embassy.org/romania/*

Russia   *www.rusembus.com/*

Rwanda   *www.rwandemb.org/*

Saudi Arabia   *www.saudi.net/*

Sierra Leone   *amenhotep4.virtualafrica.com/slmbassy/*

Slovakia   *www.slovakemb.com/*

Slovenia   *www.undp.org/missions/slovenia/*

South Africa   *www.southafrica.net/*

South Korea   *korea.emb.washington.dc.us/*

Spain   *www.spainembedu.org/*

Sri Lanka   *www.slembassy.org/*

Sweden   *www.swedenemb.org/*

Switzerland   *www.swissemb.org/*

Taiwan   *www.tw.org/*

Thailand   *www.thaiembdc.org/*

Tunisia   *www.ttmissions.com/*

Turkey   *www.turkey.org/*

Turkmenistan   *www.dc.infi.net/~embassy/*

Uganda   *www.ugandaweb.com/ugaembassy/*

Ukraine   *www.brama.com/ua-consulate/*

Uruguay   *www.embassy.org/uruguay/*

Uzbekistan   *www.uzbekistan.org/*

Vatican   *www.holyseemission.org/*

Venezuela   *venezuela.mit.edu/embassy/*

Vietnam   *www.vietnamembassy-usa.org/*

Yemen   *www.nusacc.org/yemen/*

Yugoslavia   *ourworld.compuserve.com/homepages/yuembassy/*

Zimbabwe   *www.zimweb.com/embassy/zimbabwe/*

Chapter 8

Making Contacts Through U.S. Embassies Abroad

Just as foreign countries maintain embassies and consulates within the United States, so the United States has an extensive network of diplomatic and trade embassies abroad. (Your tax dollars pay for these outposts.) Here's how you can use them to your business advantage.

Each of the embassies listed on the following pages has at least one commercial officer assigned to helping U.S. businesspeople find and strike profitable relations with other businesses or clients within the country at hand. By alerting this commercial officer to your business intentions well in advance of your visit (at least six weeks), you avail yourself of the full resources and reputation of the U.S. foreign service to help you achieve your business purposes. Using your letterhead, consider sending a fax, e-mail, or letter along the lines of this sample:

Commercial Officer
U.S. Embassy in [country name]
[address, available from the websites listed]

Dear Commercial Officer:

On [date] a business delegation [or I] will be visiting [country name] for the purpose of [describe in detail the nature of your business visit, including the names and companies of contacts you plan to make].

We would appreciate your help in [describe what you would like the commercial officer to do for you. Supply industry or association names? Provide a local business directory? Clarify license, tariff, registration, or other matters? Be available for an in-person meeting with your delegation?]

Thank you for your assistance. I can be contacted at [contact numbers inside the United States and, if available, in the country to be visited.]

Sincerely,
Your Name
Title, Company

U.S. EMBASSIES ABROAD

Arab Emirates   *www.usembabu.gov.ae/*

Argentina   *www.hq.satlink.com/usis/*

Armenia   *www.arminco.com/homepages/usis/*

Australia   *www.csccs.ozemail.com.au/~usaemb/*

Austria   *www.rpo.usia.co.at/*

Azerbaijan   *www.usia.gov/posts/baku/html*

Bahrain   *www.usembassy.com.bh/*

Bangladesh   *www.citechco.net/uskhaka/*

Barbados   *www.usia.gov/posts/bridgetown/*

Belarus   *www.usis.minsk.by/*

Belgium   *www.usinfo.be/*

Belize   *www.usemb-belize.gov/*

Benin   *eit.intnet.bj/cca/*

Bolivia   *www.negalink.com/usemblapaz/*

Botswana   *www.usia.gov/abtusia/psts/bc1/wwwhmain.html*

Brazil   *www.embaixada-americana.org.br/*

Bulgaria   *www.usis.bg/*

Canada   *www.usembassycanada.gov/*

Chile   *www.rdc.cl/~usemb/*

China   *www.redfish.com/USEmbassy-China/*

Colombia   *www.usia.gov/posts/bogota/*

Costa Rica   *www.usembassy.or.cr/*

Côte d'Ivoire   *www.usia.gov/posts/abidjan/*

Croatia   *www.open.hr/com/ae_zagreb/*

Cuba   *www.usia.gov/posts/havana/*

Cyprus   *www.americanembassy.org.cy/*

Czech Republic   *www.usis.cz/*

Denmark   *www.usis.dk/*

Dominican Republic   *www.usia.gov/posts/santodomingo/*

Ecuador   *www.usis.org.ec/*

Egypt   *www.usis.egnet.net/*

El Salvador   *www.usinfo.org.sv/*

Eritrea   *www.usia.gov/posts/eritrea/*

Estonia   *www.usislib.ee/usislib/*

Finland   *www.usis.fi/*

France   *www.amb-usa.fr/*

Georgia   *www.sanet.ge.usis/mission.html*

Germany   *www.usia.gov/posts/bonn.html*

Ghana   *www.usembassy.org.gh/*

Great Britain   *www.usembassy.org.uk/*

Greece   *www.usisathen.gr/usisathens/*

Grenada   *www.spiceisle.com/homepages/usemb_gd/*

Guinea   *www.eti-bull.net/usembassy/*

Hungary   *www.usis.hu/*

Iceland   *www.itn.is/america/*

India   *www.usia.gov/posts/delhi.html*

Indonesia   *www.usembassyjakarta.org/*

Ireland   *www.indigo.ie/usembassy-usis/*

Israel   *www.usis-israel.org.il/*

Italy   *www.usis.it/*

Japan   *www.usia.gov/posts/japan/*

Jordan   *www.usia.gov/posts/amman/*

Korea   *www.usia.gov/posts/seoul/*

Kuwait   *www.kuwait.net/~usiskwt/wwwhemb.htm*

Laos   *www.inet.co.th/org/usis/laos.htm*

Latvia   *www.usis.bkc.lv/*

Lebanon   *www.usembassy.com.lb/*

Lesotho   *www.lesoff.co.za/amemb/embassy.html*

Lithuania   *www.usis.lt/*

Luxembourg   *www.usia.gov/posts/luxembourg.html*

Malaysia   *www.jaring.my/usiskl/*

Mali   *www.malinet.nl/cca/*

Malta   *www.usia.gov/posts/malta.html*

Mauritius   *usis.intnet.mu/*

Mexico   *www.usembassy.org.mx/*

Moldova   *usis.moldnet.md/*

Mozambique   *www.info.usaid.gov/mz/*

Nepal   *www.south-asia.com/USA/*

Netherlands   *www.usemb.nl/*

New Zealand   *www.usia.gov/posts/wellington/*

Nicaragua   *www.usaid.org.ni/*

Nigeria   *www.gsi-niger.com/cca-usis/*

Norway   *www.usembassy.no/*

Oman   *www.usia.gov/posts/muscat/*

Pakistan   *www.usia.gov/posts/karachi/*

Palestine   *www.info.usaid.gov/wbg/*

Panama   *www.pty.com/usispan/*

Peru   *www.rcp.net.pe/usa/*

Philippines   *www.usaid-ph.gov/*

Poland   *www.usaemb.pl/*

Portugal   *www.portugal.doc.gov/*

Qatar   *www.qatar.net.usisdoha/*

Romania   *www.usis.ro/*

Russia   *www.usia.gov/posts/moscow.html*

Senegal   *www.usia.gov/abtusia/posts/SG1/wwwhemb.html*

Singapore   *home1.pacific.net.dg/~amemb/*

Slovakia   *www.usis.sk/*

South Africa   *www.usia.gov/posts/pretoria/*

Spain   *www.embusa.es/*

Sri Lanka   *www.usia.gov/posts/sri_lanka/*

Sweden   *www.usis.usemb.se/*

Switzerland   *www.itu.int/embassy/us/*

Taiwan   *www.ait.org.tw/*

Thailand   *www.usa.or.th/*

Turkey   *www.usis-ankara.org.tr/*

Ukraine   *www.usemb.kiev.ua/*

Uruguay   *www.embeeuu.gub.uy/*

Uzbekistan   *www.freenet.uz/usis/*

Venezuela   *www.usia.gov/posts/caracas/*

Vietnam   *members.aol.com/nomhawj/embassy/home.htm*

Yugoslavia   *www.amembbg.co.yu/*

Zambia   *www.zamnet.zm/zamnet/usemb/*

Chapter 9

Excellent Reference Reading for 30 Trading Nations

Argentina

J.L. Nolan. *Argentina Business: The Portable Encyclopedia for Doing Business with Argentina* (1998).

Australia

P. North, B. Toews. *Succeed in Business: Australia* (1998).

Brazil
R.C. Kelly. *Country Review: Brazil* (1999).

Canada
J. Whittle, A. Woznick, et al. *Canada Business* (1997).

China
Y.C. Wang. *Investment in China: A Question and Answer Guide* (1997).

Egypt
S. Wilson. *Culture Shock: Egypt* (1998).

France
C. Gordon, P. Kingston. *The Business Culture in France* (1996).

Germany
R. Flamini, B. Szerlip. *Passport Germany: Your Pocket Guide to German Business, Customs & Etiquette* (1997).

Great Britain
P. Kenna, S. Lacy. *Business U.K.* (1996).

Greece
E.T. Rossides, S.B. Hadji, et al. *Doing Business in Greece: A Legal and Practical Reference Guide* (1997).

Hong Kong
A. Grzeskowiak, T. Watson, et al. *Passport Hong Kong* (1996).

India

M. Joshi, B. Szerlip. *Passport India* (1997).

Indonesia

M. Sinjorgo. *Succeed in Business: Indonesia* (1998).

Ireland

A. McNamara. *Simple Guide to Customs and Etiquette in Ireland* (1998).

Israel

D. Rosenthal, et al. *Passport Israel* (1996).

Italy

P. Kenna, S. Lacy. *Business Italy: A Practical Guide to Understanding Italian Business Culture* (1994).

Japan

American Chamber of Commerce in Japan. *A Guide to Doing Business in Japan* (1996).

Korea

P. Kenna, S. Lacy, *Business Korea: A Practical Guide to Understanding South Korean Business* (1997).

Malaysia

G. Brooks, V. Brooks. *Malaysia: A Kick Start Guide for Business Travelers* (1996).

Mexico

G. Newman, A. Szterenfeld. *Business International's Guide to Doing Business in Mexico* (1998).

Morocco
G. Evans. *Smart Business Morocco: What to Expect and Do When Doing Business with the Moroccans* (1997).

Netherlands
H. Janin. *Culture Shock: Netherlands* (1998).

Norway
E. Su-Dale. *Culture Shock: Norway* (1996).

Philippines
E. Hinkelman. *Philippines Business* (1998).

Russia
M. Bosrock. *Put Your Best Foot Forward: Russia* (1996).

Saudi Arabia
A. Shoult. *Doing Business in Saudi Arabia* (1999).

Singapore
C. Genzberger, et al. *Singapore Business* (1996).

South Africa
J. Reuvid, et al. *Doing Business in South Africa* (1998).

Spain
P. Villanueva, R. Bennett. *Doing Business with Spain* (1997).

Sri Lanka
D. Bullis. *Culture Shock: Sri Lanka* (1997).

Sweden

C.R. Svensson, C. Rosen. *Culture Shock: Sweden* (1997).

Taiwan

M. Clancy. *Business Guide to Taiwan* (1999).

Thailand

P. Leppert. *Doing Business with Thailand* (1997).

Ukraine

A. Jolly, N. Kitten. *Doing Business in the Ukraine* (1998).

Vietnam

J.E. Curry, et al. *Passport Vietnam: Your Pocket Guide to Vietnamese Business, Customs & Etiquette* (1997).

Chapter 10

Organizations
Providing
Cross-Cultural
Training for
Business

Several companies offer cross-cultural training for individuals and groups. Although the following list is not intended as an endorsement, we urge firms to consider working with professional guidance in developing and delivering cross-cultural training suited to their specific needs.

www.global-integration.com/
This company discusses and provides education concerning the major dilemmas facing people working within truly international or global corporations. Global Integration's programs are designed

to develop the specific knowledge, skills, and processes needed to resolve what they consider to be the four main barriers to international effectiveness: distance, culture, time, and technology.

www.worldbiz.com/CGAexpatriate.html
This company offers assistance in the assessment and selection of expatriation candidates; training for large and small groups of expatriates or expatriation candidates; preparation for American managers and colleagues of soon-to-arrive expats from abroad; teamwork facilitation workshops for multicultural working groups; and programs for expats living and working in Europe (other world regions being added).

www.worldbiz.com/index.html
This company is a source of information on international business practices, international business protocol, international etiquette, cross-cultural communication, negotiating tactics, and country-specific data.

www.cultureinteraction.com/
This company helps people manage the interplay of cultures in their work environment. The purpose of Culture Interaction is to develop you and your colleagues' or employees' intercultural knowledge and skills, so that you can better handle situations in which you are unaware of the rules of the game. Programs encourage cross-cultural self-sufficiency, so that clients are prepared to approach whatever cultural challenges they encounter.

www/global-dynamics.com/
This international consulting firm designs, organizes, and implements cross-cultural and general management training programs

worldwide. Working towards more efficiency and success in the culturally diverse marketplace, they offer training in international human resource development, international management, team building, curriculum design, strategic planning, benchmark studies, organizational development, international marketing, and international trade show analysis.

www.worldbiz.com/ITAPtraining.html

These practical training programs offer strategies that can be applied immediately in the new workplace and country, thus improving productivity and effectiveness while increasing the employee's family's comfort level with their new situation. Programs are customized to meet the specific needs of each company and relocation situation.

www.worldbiz.com/morey_manor.html

This is a trade and consulting organization that helps businesses to capture new markets and opportunities through strategic alliances in order to achieve international expansion objectives.

www.sococo.com/

This training and consulting firm is dedicated to building bridges of understanding between cultures (mostly the American and French cultures). Programs are offered for individuals as well as corporations.

www.berlitz.com/cross_cultural/cross_cultural.html

Berlitz Cross-Cultural Training programs are designed to bridge cultural gaps for international travelers as well as for business transferees and their families. These programs provide important information regarding daily life, social and business do's and don'ts, how to communicate and negotiate better across cultures, how to manage more effectively with people of other countries, and other miscellaneous topics.

www/rowlandandassociates.com/class.htm
This firm specializes in cultural awareness and skill training for countries in Latin America, Europe, the Middle East, Russia/CIS, as well as Japan, China, and other Asia/Pacific countries. Services are provided by a team of handpicked professional trainers and consultants chosen for their cultural expertise, their presentation skills, and their ability to convey complex concepts in practical language.

www.comcul.com/cciccts.html
This firm has cross-cultural training seminars and consultation geared towards Japan. It offers predeparture orientation seminars, debriefing/reentry orientation seminars, and other services for corporations doing business with the Japanese.

www.bwvideo.com/index.htm
Here you will find a wide selection of videos useful for training in international business topics.

www.japanbusinessgroup.com/Cross_Cultural_Consulting.html
The Japan Business Group offers to train employees to work effectively within the context of Japanese management hierarchy and the Japanese corporate structure.

INDEX